# How to Therapize and Heal Yourself:
## *15 Self-Therapy Techniques to Understand Your Past and Control Your Future*

By Nick Trenton
www.nicktrenton.com

# Table of Contents

**HOW TO THERAPIZE AND HEAL YOURSELF: *15 SELF-THERAPY TECHNIQUES TO UNDERSTAND YOUR PAST AND CONTROL YOUR FUTURE***     1

**TABLE OF CONTENTS**     3

**CHAPTER 1: UNDERSTANDING THOUGHTS, BELIEFS, AND BEHAVIORS**     5

PART 1: COGNITIVE BEHAVIORAL THERAPY     7
PART 2: BEHAVIORAL ACTIVATION     19
PART 3: UNDERSTANDING CORE BELIEFS—AND REWRITING THEM     31
PART 4: OPPOSITE ACTION     44

**CHAPTER 2: UNDERSTANDING WHAT YOU'RE MADE OF**     61

PART 1: SELF-QUESTIONING     61
PART 2: DELVING INTO THE SHADOWS     73
PART 3: UNDERSTANDING AVOIDANCE MECHANISMS     86
PART 4: GESTALT TECHNIQUES—THE EMPTY CHAIR     97

# CHAPTER 3: WHERE IT ALL CAME FROM  111

**PART 1: WHAT IS YOUR ATTACHMENT STYLE?**  112
**PART 2: REPARENTING YOURSELF**  126
**PART 3: TRANSACTIONAL ANALYSIS**  138

# CHAPTER 4: ANXIETY, TRAUMA, AND COPING  154

**PART 1: COGNITIVE DEFUSION EXERCISES**  154
**PART 2: THE ART OF "COPING AHEAD"**  167
**PART 3: SYSTEMATIC DESENSITIZATION**  176
**PART 4: THE REWIND TECHNIQUE**  187

## SUMMARY GUIDE  201

# Chapter 1: Understanding Thoughts, Beliefs, and Behaviors

Have you ever found yourself behaving in a certain way but not really knowing *why*? Do you have a tendency to lash out emotionally or say and do things that you later regret? Have you ever asked yourself how you feel or what you want, only to hear the answer *I don't know*?

If so, then this is the book for you. In the chapters that follow, we'll explore the root causes of all those behaviors in life that sabotage our happiness and undermine our wellbeing. Whether it's poor communication in relationships, addictions, unmanaged anxiety and depression, or simply a constant feeling that you're not living to your fullest potential, there is usually one predictable root cause behind it all: **lack of awareness**.

Traditionally, a psychologist or psychotherapist could help you more deeply understand who you are, what you want, and how you tick. But if that's not a possibility for you, rest assured that you can master the very same techniques for yourself and become your own therapist. Throughout this book, we'll look at the lives of fictional people who are all experiencing very different life challenges, yet in their own way, each of them has just one problem—a lack of awareness of their emotions, core beliefs, blind spots, and expectations.

As you read, you'll be invited to look more closely at your own emotions, thoughts, and beliefs, and how they are motivating certain behaviors and habits. Being your own therapist doesn't take any magical skill or superhuman ability. All it takes is the willingness to be honest, to ask questions, and to courageously take action according to the insights you glean. Let's jump in.

## Part 1: Cognitive Behavioral Therapy

Meet Clara. Going about her life one day, she encounters two particular situations.

<u>Situation 1</u> is that she receives an email from a work colleague asking her a question about a presentation she gave two weeks earlier. She reads the email, understands the question, and answers it factually.

<u>Situation 2</u> is that Clara gets home from work and sees that her husband hasn't arrived home yet. She immediately thinks, "He's been in a car crash and he's dead." Terrified, she immediately takes action by blowing up his phone with panicky messages, then furiously Googles "how to plan a funeral."

Later, she feels a little ashamed of how over-the-top her actions were.

What is the difference between these situations? In both, Clara is having a cognitive response to some stimulus in the environment. Yet in Situation 2, it's clear that her thoughts about the situation *are not helpful or accurate*. In fact, it's not the situation itself that compels Clara to feel and act as she does, but rather her thoughts about the situation.

This is the key insight behind cognitive behavioral therapy, or CBT: **that not all of our thoughts are for our benefit. Thoughts, feelings, and actions are all connected.** The way we think about things affects how we feel, and how we feel affects how we act. How we act, in turn, changes our world in ways that confirm or reinforce how we think or feel.

The American Psychological Association (APA) explains that there are three core concepts behind CBT:

1. Psychological problems are caused at least in part by unhelpful or inaccurate ways of thinking.
2. Psychological problems are also caused in part by maladaptive (i.e., not useful or healthy) behavior patterns and habits—and many of these are themselves caused by our thinking.
3. Because we learned how to think in these maladaptive ways, we can *unlearn* them. In other words, if we hope to address our psychological problems, we can do so by starting with the maladaptive thoughts that underpin those problems.

The idea is that if you can become **aware** of your thought patterns and how they're affecting your life, then you can take steps to change them for the better. Without awareness, old habits keep playing out and patterns keep repeating themselves. We'll learn more about Clara throughout the chapters of this book, as well as three other people who are experiencing mental health difficulties that you may recognize in yourself. For Clara, CBT is a way to get a handle on her anxious thought patterns so that she can control them rather than them controlling her. But CBT has also been proven to help when it comes to

- Depression
- PTSD
- Stress management
- Self-esteem issues
- Eating disorders
- Anger management
- Chronic Pain

Basically, if your thoughts are involved at any point, then CBT can help. But before we go on, it's worth understanding that CBT (and indeed all the techniques we'll explore in the chapters that follow) is not a silver bullet. It's not for everyone or all problems, at all times. What it can do, however, is help you gain awareness of the cognitive component of your own mental health issues so that you can make changes. This is a theme we'll keep returning to: No single theory is "right" or the solution; rather, it's the awareness and self-mastery that we gain by using this or that technique that really matters.

**In CBT, the goal is to take automatic, negative, unhelpful, and unconscious thoughts and deliberately transform them into conscious, helpful ones that allow you to live the kind of life you want to live**. If you're reading this book, chances are that there is something in your life right now that is causing you distress, yet you don't have a firm handle on it. Using CBT and the other techniques we'll explore, you will learn

1. How to slow down and become aware of the difference between situations, thoughts, feelings, and actions/behaviors
2. What your core beliefs are and how they play out in your life
3. To challenge and replace your irrational beliefs and sabotaging assumptions

4. How to spot bad mental habits and cognitive distortions and take control

Just like Clara, some of your thoughts day to day will be neutral, accurate, helpful, and realistic. But some of them won't be. If we wish to become our own therapists, where do we start? After all, if our thinking itself is distorted, how can we trust it to help us solve that very same distortion?

Bear in mind that cognitive distortions are normal. Everyone has them. They only become a problem when we fail to recognize them as distortions. This is the power of CBT—**we learn that we don't have to believe everything we think**. What we can do is stop, become aware, and notice what we are thinking. Then, we can hold that thought up to the light and really look at it. Is it true? Is it helpful? Does it inspire the kind of action that will create the life we want? Does it feel good, and does it align with our values?

Maybe we find out that the thought is a pretty good one, after all, and we keep it. But if we discover that a thought is truly not serving us, we empower ourselves to make different choices.

## How to Spot a Cognitive Distortion

A cognitive distortion only *feels* like the truth. It feels like we are neutrally observing reality—but we're not. Take a look at some common distortions and see if you have ever entertained thoughts of this kind in your own life before.

**All-or-nothing thinking**, where we see only in black-or-white extreme terms instead of the more likely grey areas in between. "She said she wasn't interested in dating me, so obviously she hates me."

**Should statements**, where we labor under some assumptions about what we ought to be doing and the rules we ought to be following. "I don't know why I'm so uncertain at the moment; I should be happy!"

**Catastrophizing**, where we assume the worst possible outcome is the one that will happen. "If I lose my job, I'll never find another one and I'll be destitute and forced to beg on the streets . . ."

**Overgeneralization**, where we assume that one observation applies to other unrelated situations. "She didn't want to date me, so that means nobody ever will."

**Filtering**, where we interpret neutral or positive events through a negative lens and come to some preconceived conclusions. "She said she'd go out with me . . . so I guess that means she feels sorry for me."

Closely related is **discounting the positive**, where we ignore the good and focus heavily on the bad. "I don't care that most judges gave me a perfect score—why did that one judge only give me a nine out of ten? What did I do wrong?"

**Mindreading**, where we assume we know what others think and feel, without any evidence. "I have to host Christmas every year; people expect it and would be so disappointed in me if I stopped."

**Personalization**, where we put ourselves at the center of things and assume that we are responsible for things that really have nothing to do with us. "My son is failing chemistry, and I feel like it's my fault for not supporting him better."

And so on. In fact, there are probably as many types of cognitive distortions as there are thoughts! Clara has a thought that is catastrophizing ("he's had a car crash"), which she wholly believes in the moment. But she can recognize this as a distortion by stopping and becoming aware of her **thoughts as thoughts** and not automatically assuming that every thought is true. Then she can deliberately challenge her thoughts and *consciously choose* what to think, behave, and feel.

This process of deliberately engaging with our thoughts is called **cognitive restructuring**, and it's a popular CBT technique. It's not dissimilar to becoming aware that you are looking at life through a filter or a lens. CBT lets you ask what kind of image you're seeing, whether it's distorted or not, and whether you can put a different lens on the camera entirely. Here's how.

**Step 1: Become aware**

Cognitive distortions have power because we're unaware of them. The first step, then, is to notice them happening when they happen. A good clue that your thinking is distorted is a feeling of disproportionate response, i.e., if you feel that you're suddenly emotional without really understanding why, become curious about what assumptions you're habitually falling into. Don't assume that it will be easy to spot your thoughts at first—it takes practice and honesty!

One way is to deliberately pause every time you feel upset, angry, confused, etc. Slow down and sit quietly somewhere with a journal and write down your thoughts. Don't censor yourself or get carried away with blame or shame.

Clara might write a stream of thoughts that looks like this: "He never comes home late from work. It doesn't make any sense that he would, so I'm sure that something must have happened. That's the only thing that can explain in this situation. And I'm all alone here, and I have no idea what I'd do if something happened to him . . . I can't even think of how I would go on if I knew he was gone . . ." And so on.

**Step 2: Appraise**

Take a step back and look at the thoughts. Ask yourself:

*Can I recognize any distortion here?*

*Do I have any real evidence for this conclusion?*

*Is there potentially another way of looking at this?*

Naturally, this takes some willingness to be honest. Clara might zoom in on the thought "there's no other explanation for his lateness" and ask herself if she knows this to be factually and logically true. She considers alternatives. He might have been in a car crash, sure, but he also might be stuck in traffic or was asked last minute to stay at work. He may have taken a detour to pick up Clara's favorite takeout for dinner that evening!

Do the same and ask yourself about the quality of these thoughts. How do they make you feel? What actions do they inspire? Now look at these feelings and actions and ask if they are what you want for yourself. If not, then deliberately tell yourself (try actually saying it out loud to yourself) that **it's just a thought, and a thought can be changed**.

**Step 3: Reframe**

No, it is impossible to change the world just by changing our thoughts. But we can always change our *perspective* on that world, how we frame things, our interpretations, our focus, and the filter we place over what we see. Is there an upside or benefit you're ignoring? Are you treating certain assumptions as true when they aren't? Try to imagine what your perspective looks like without those assumptions.

Clara, once she noticed how awful she feels when she believes her distorted thought ("he's dead!") and how much she dislikes the behavior it causes, tells herself that there *is* an explanation for her husband's lateness, but she doesn't know what it is right now, and that's okay. She tries on a few perspectives, asking herself questions and challenging her assumptions. After a little internal dialogue with herself, Clara feels calmer as she thinks, "It's certainly unusual that he's late, but I have no idea what's happening, so there's no point in getting anxious."

A nagging, persistent voice tells her, "But what if he *is* dead, though?" and Clara looks at this, realizing that it, too, is just a thought, and she can pause, become aware of it, appraise it, and deliberately choose to listen to it or not. She dismisses this thought. She can see an anxious detour that this thought is inviting her to take, but it doesn't mean she has to go down that path. Five minutes later, her husband turns up at home—he had a puncture but it's all fixed now.

You might be thinking that CBT must only be useful for simple situations like Clara's, but the beauty of the technique is that it can be applied to all sorts of mental distortions, big or small, temporary or long lasting. For example, Clara might try therapizing herself with this CBT technique in small ways, but in the longer term, she starts to notice far-reaching effects. She begins to be aware of her tendency to catastrophize in all sorts of situations.

Though "rewriting" a simple thought doesn't seem like much, these small changes start to make big shifts in Clara's life. One day, her husband casually suggests she apply for a big fancy job that's opened up with twice the pay and plenty of interesting perks. Clara immediately dismisses the idea, but then stops and thinks, *why?* She practices the same process of pausing to become aware, appraising her thoughts and then moving ahead in conscious awareness, and notices for the first time how quickly she turns down a challenge. When she examines her thoughts, she realizes it all comes down to catastrophizing.

In the past, she wouldn't have even noticed herself thinking the thought, "Don't bother trying that; it'll never work out for you. It'll be a disaster . . ." yet all the same, it would influence her actions and how she felt about herself. But with the increased **awareness** that this CBT technique is teaching her, she can pull these unconscious assumptions out into the light and ask whether they're really working for her. In this way, the simple technique of cognitive reframing can have deep and lasting effects on your life.

**Part 2: Behavioral Activation**

Remember, however, that thoughts are just one part of the puzzle.

Let's now look at Nick, who would tell you in no uncertain terms that he is depressed. Nick has plenty of distorted thoughts.

*I'm not good at anything.*

*There's no point in trying; I'll probably just fail anyway.*

*I don't care about anything, and nothing makes me happy anymore.*

He tries his best to challenge these thoughts. He tells himself that he is good at some things, that he should keep putting himself out there, keep trying new stuff, and reminding himself of his blessings. It doesn't work. Why?

Let's take a closer look at Nick's life. He lives at home in a cramped room. He hates cleaning the place up, so he procrastinates, and the place gets steadily worse until he can't bear it and feels ashamed about the mess. He's overweight, but every time he goes to the gym, he realizes just how out of shape he is. It seems like it takes three days to recover from even a basic workout session, so he quickly loses motivation, beating himself up for being such a lazy weakling.

He needs to find a better job so he can move out, but every time he looks at his resume, he wants to scream. So he puts that off, too. He used to get a lot of joy out of his hobbies and meeting up with friends, but he can't be bothered with any of that now. In fact, all he seems to have time for now is junk food, gaming (which he doesn't really enjoy, anyway), and watching TV. Pretty grim, right?

Nick's problem is that when he says, "I just don't care anymore," this is not really a cognitive distortion—he's correct! At the same time, how can he genuinely convince himself to reframe his thoughts ("I'm a talented individual with plenty to offer and I enjoy my life") when his room is a pigsty, he's unfit and sixty pounds overweight, and he's wasting six hours every day zoned out in front of screens? He might believe it for a little while, but not for long.

Clearly he needs an approach that's very different from Clara's.

In the 1970s, Peter Lewinsohn and his research team at the University of Oregon came up with a way to treat depression called "behavioral activation." Lewinsohn was influenced by behaviorism, which is the understanding that your environment has an enormous effect on how you act. This is not to say that thoughts and feelings don't feature—only that they're not the only thing that counts. In general, behaviorism rests on two main tenets.

**When you get a reward for something, you're likely to do it again.** If you cook for people you care about and they tell you how good it is, you'll probably want to cook again and maybe even get better at it.

**When you get in trouble for something, you tend to stop doing it.** If you cook for people you care about and they criticize you and your food, it's understandable that you might not want to try again.

B.F. Skinner, a well-known behaviorist, thought that a person gets depressed when their environment punishes them too much and gives them too few rewards. To put it another way, it can be hard to get motivated to do much of anything when everything seems hard or painful. Depression can cause physical symptoms like tiredness and changes in energy, which can also play a role. Depression can make you think that no matter what you do, you will fail.

But you can probably see the issue with Nick—the less he does, the lower his sense of accomplishment, so the less he gets done. The less he takes care of his health, the harder it is to get fit again. Going to the gym, then, is a painful experience that yields very little benefit—at least not at first. If he was fit, going to the gym may feel like a pleasant and rewarding experience. But he's not, so he's increasingly less inclined to do it.

Depression, understood in these terms, is simply a case of *momentum*. It's hard to change the way you think if nothing changes in your life.

What's the way out of this horrible spiral? **Behavioral activation has you do something to feel better instead of waiting until you feel better to do something**. Behavioral activation for depression is about making your life meaningful and pleasurable again. It involves these steps:

1. Activity monitoring
2. Value setting
3. Activity scheduling
4. Troubleshooting

Let's look at each in turn and how Nick could use them to steadily crawl out of his hole of depression. Remember how Clara began her process of cognitive restructuring by just becoming aware? It's the same for Nick. The first step is for him to just understand what is actually happening for him in his life as it is now.

## Activity Monitoring

First, Nick gathers data on how he spends his time. **Instead of monitoring thoughts, he is monitoring actions and behaviors** via looking at his day-to-day activities. Using an Excel spreadsheet of his own design (you can find readymade activity sheets online, if you like), he records everything he does for a full week.

Every hour—including sleep—he notes what activities he does. No activity is too small or obvious or insignificant. While he does this, Nick also records his overall mood. This is done by simply noting hour by hour where his mood falls on a scale of one to ten.

At the end of the week, Nick has some valuable data to explore. Reviewing the chart, he can start to see patterns. He asks himself:

*What was I doing when I felt the best? And when I felt the worst?*

*What is the overall relationship between my activity levels and my mood?*

*How did I feel on days when I was very inactive—for example, not leaving the house, not showering, or not tidying up?*

Now, Nick can compile a list of activities that he knows make him feel good—he has the concrete evidence! He can draw up a "feel good" list as well as a "feel bad" one. His "feel good" list might contain the following items:

- Taking a walk and getting some fresh air
- Spending time with friends
- Doing a hobby

His "feel bad" list includes these items:

- Staying in bed past 10 a.m.
- Gaming
- Scrolling social media in bed with the lights off

Now, all of the above may seem pretty obvious to you and me, but the truth is that when we can see in black and white how our mood literally rises and falls without our activity level, it can create a few lightbulb moments. If you try this yourself, you might also be surprised at a few things that you thought made you feel good but don't, and vice versa.

**Value Setting**

Now, in just the same way that Clara became curious about cognitive alternatives, Nick is going to ask himself about activity/behavioral alternatives. For Clara, a thought is appraised as a good one when it is healthy, rational, accurate, and so on. But how can Nick determine which behaviors to keep and which to change? The answer is: his values.

You might think—isn't the fact of his negative mood the real hint? The truth is, **we all feel low when we are not living according to our values**. So, we can take depression, lack of motivation, etc. as symptoms of a bigger problem—our living out of alignment with what we value. Engage in those activities that flow from your values, the theory goes, and you gradually pull yourself out of the spiral of negativity. Trying to address the negativity alone is like trying to correct the course of a ship without knowing which direction you are wanting to go in the first place.

Only you can decide what your values are. They will not be the same as other people's—in fact, they can change over time even for you. What do you think is most important in life? What is the ideal way that you want to interact with others, behave, think, see yourself? It's not being able to achieve these ideals that makes us happy.

We can live meaningful and rich lives simply by understanding what we value and knowing that we are working each day toward those values. This gives purpose, direction, motivation, dignity, and resilience.

Pause and ask what you most value about being alive right now. Then read the following list and see which ones speak to you most.

**Family** – be it tradition, loving connection, duty, or simply a sense of belonging. It could mean mastering the task of parenthood and serving others.

**Romantic love** – that could mean a successful marriage, passion, commitment, or a deep and transcendent bond with another person.

**Community, friendship, and social life** – a different kind of love, but no less powerful.

**Spirituality or religion** – do you value contemplation, the mystical or inner life, a union with God, or a spiritual and personal development path all your own creation?

**Learning and knowledge** – the love of developing understanding and mastery.

**Material stability, wealth, financial success** – yes, it's okay to have this as a value!

**Beauty, poetry, art** – are you supremely driven by aesthetic concerns?

There is not really a fixed list of human values. What's important is to make sure that they're really *your* values—not your parents', not your social group's, and not something you were told you should want by the media, for example. Perhaps you choose three things that are most important to you. Stuck? A great way to home in on values is to ask

*When have I felt most satisfied/alive/happy/myself? What value was being met at that moment?*

*If I could achieve just one thing during my time on earth, what would it be?*

*Think of someone you completely dislike and disagree with—what is the opposite value? What does this dislike tell you about what you find most important?*

For Nick, honest contemplation tells him that he most values independence, honesty, and kindness. Those are the principles he wants to build his life around.

## Activity Scheduling

Behavioral activation is all about what you *do*, though—not just what you think and feel. Now, write down a list of activities that you can practically do, and think of this as a kind of recipe for certain good feelings. Choose activities based on what you already know feels good (from when you monitored yourself earlier), but also activities that speak to your values.

Nick decides that he will add to his "feel good" list the following activities:

*Volunteer with kids at his community center*

*Book a therapy session*

*Start exploring options for creating his own business*

He notices that just writing these down gives him a jolt of energy—a good sign that they speak to a person's needs and values!

Now, Nick can start building his life from scratch one activity at a time. He looks at a schedule and plans every hour. He makes sure to include the basics (sleep, grooming, time for meals, etc.) but *prioritizes* those activities he already knows speak to his values and make him feel good. That's important—these activities are scheduled in first!

**He decides what he'll do, when he will do it, for how long, where, and who with.** He is keenly aware of *why* he is doing it—nothing external is forcing him; rather, he is doing it because it will help him achieve what he wants to achieve. Nick also finds it helpful to rank activities on a hierarchy—some are better for him than others. He also ranks them by how difficult they are to do. You guessed it—he chooses the activities that yield the greatest number of positive feelings while costing him the least motivation. That way, he builds momentum, generating good feelings that he can then re-invest into other, more energetically "expensive" activities.

Every Sunday evening, he plans his week ahead, down to the hour. He doesn't see this as a chore—after all, he knows that if he gets it right, the outcome will be plenty of happy, satisfied feelings.

**Troubleshooting**

Does Nick manage to change his life completely after one week? Of course not! But he diligently appraises how it went and makes adjustments. He knows that being depressed distorts his view on things, so he gives each activity a fair try—at least twice—before deciding he doesn't want to do it. When he doesn't stick to his plan, he doesn't beat himself up or throw the whole schedule out the window. He just becomes curious about why it didn't work, and asks himself what *will* work and what he can do for next time.

The interesting thing about Nick is that only once he makes headway with his activity schedule in this way, and maintains that momentum for a few months, is he able to start looking at his thoughts and feelings like Clara did. Once Nick creates a healthier, more supportive environment for himself, he is naturally more able to spot—and challenge—his cognitive distortions.

## Part 3: Understanding Core Beliefs—and Rewriting Them

We saw that Clara had a problem with anxiety and catastrophic thinking. For Nick, depression was the problem. For both of them, we can understand their thoughts as smaller leaves branching off a tree. But what kind of tree is it? Your core beliefs are like the main trunk of a tree, out of which all your more superficial thoughts branch out and grow.

Clara's "leaves" are plentiful:

*"Don't get too comfy because that's when trouble will hit!"*

*"You can't trust anyone but yourself."*

*"This is obviously not going to work out for you."*

But feeding all these thoughts is a core belief, the trunk of the tree: "I am not safe."

For Nick, his "leaves" are equally as plentiful:

*"I'm a loser."*

*"That's fine for other people, but I could never do that."*

*"How could a therapist possibly help me?"*

Feeding all of these thoughts is a central trunk: "I am not enough."

**Core beliefs are deeply held ideas that influence how we behave, how we see ourselves, and how we understand the world around us**. These ideas affect **everything**—how we feel, what we think, what we choose and don't choose, how we interpret the world, how we explain it to ourselves, and indeed, the entire narrative we construct to make sense of all the events in our lives. Our core beliefs are an intrinsic fundamental part of who we are—like our name or where we were born.

However, there's one way in which they're different—we can change them. Is it difficult? Yes. Extremely. But it is possible, and if you can change your core beliefs, you can change your life. You could constantly pluck away at the leaves that grow on your tree, but if the trunk is always there, those leaves will keep growing just the same.

Working on core beliefs, then, is a question of the *level* you're addressing your problem at. Change your deep core beliefs, and you automatically change everything that happens at shallower levels. Superficial change often doesn't last because it leaves the underlying core beliefs intact. So, if, for example, Nick truly believes that he is not enough, any momentary praise or validation will not "stick." Until he genuinely changes his belief and starts to think, "I am a good person. I have value and I am enough," then he will continue to think, feel, and behave as he always has.

Beliefs are just thoughts that we tell ourselves over and over again and think are true. That's it. They're not set in stone. They're just stories you've told over and over and over again. A belief can be a simple idea, like "life is hard," or it can be a complex set of ideas and statements—an entire belief system.

Whether you know it or not, you are always confirming this belief system. In fact, if you really listen to yourself, you are always defending the "rightness" of your beliefs, even if they hurt your happiness and wellbeing. That's the purpose of the cognitive distortions we identified above—they act as constant filters, shaping reality so it fits the idea we already have of it.

**The Downward Arrow Technique**

If you steadily increase your own levels of awareness, it's only a matter of time before you start spotting recurring patterns. If you do as Clara did and become an expert at reframing your own thoughts, you may start to notice that they all share the same "flavor." Core beliefs are often very simple but powerful. You may be surprised to know that while everyone's "leaves" differ wildly, core beliefs tend to drill down to some very predictable and stable human patterns:

*I am not enough.*

*There is not enough (i.e., things are scarce, and I have to fight for everything I have).*

*The world is a bad place.*

*People cannot be trusted.*

*I am a bad person.*

*There is something wrong with me.*

*Life will always be unfair.*

*Things cannot really change.*

*I am unlike everyone else.*

*Life is fundamentally a game you can't win.*

*I am a victim.*

*I have to be in control.*

If you're still getting acquainted with the deeper core-belief programming running in your own life, here's a useful exercise to start narrowing things down further: the downward arrow technique.

You begin by becoming aware of and challenging the negative habitual thoughts you have, then ask yourself WHY it would bother you if it were true. Instead of taking your assumptions at face value, you keep drilling down to find the belief underpinning everything. Three questions you can keep asking yourself:

**"What does this mean to me?"**
**"Even if this were accurate, why is it such a big deal?"**
**"What are you afraid of?"**

Here's how the technique might look with an example. Thea has just retired from a successful and illustrious career, but has found herself hitting a wall, psychologically speaking. She's at a time in her life where she is taking a really honest look at her values, her identity, and what she really wants for her life. At a time when she should be celebrating her wins and relaxing into her later years, she finds she is riddled with negativity. So, she sets to work digging in to find her core beliefs.

**Step 1: Become aware of a negative and automatic thought**

One day, Thea is out having breakfast in a café on a weekday and notices that most people around her are either old or stay-at-home moms out with their children. She catches the almost-instant thought, "I'm bunking. I should be doing something useful with my life." Thea only recognizes this thought because she notices the sudden drop in mood she feels. She slows down and looks at this thought and even jots it down in a journal so she can look at it more closely.

## Step 2: Question that thought

Imagine that every thought you've ever had has deep roots that, if you followed them, would carry you all the way down to a core belief—if you kept questioning it, that is. Thea asks herself the three questions above. She then questions the very answers she gives, continuing on.

"I'm bunking. I should be doing something useful with my life."

*What does "bunking" mean to you?*

"It means being a useless human. It means shirking your responsibilities and not being productive."

*Not being productive—why is that such a big deal?*

"It's a big deal because if you're not being a valuable member of society, then what are you?"

*What does that mean to you, "valuable member of society"?*

"It means you work. You earn your place."

*What are you afraid of?*

"I don't want to be that person, someone who is useless."

*Even if you were useless, would that be such a big deal?*

"Yes?"

*Why? What does it mean to be useless?*

"It means that you will be discarded."

After a while, Thea starts to converge on something that feels profound. Her core belief goes something like this: *Unless I am providing value for others, then I have no value.* If Thea digs even deeper, she may find a more fundamental belief still, i.e., that she is essentially worthless as she is. That's why she believes that she has to *earn* her worth—through work.

Thea knows that she's on to something with this belief because, once she identifies it, it's like she can see it everywhere! She starts to notice how this main belief feeds into so many assumptions, biases, expectations, and attitudes. A core belief is not a sentence or phrase so much as it is a *feeling*. Many of us instill our core beliefs way before we even learn to speak, and that means they are pre-verbal, maybe even symbolic. We can express our beliefs in many different ways, but what matters is the feeling it conjures for us. The root is psychological and emotional, not verbal—so don't worry too much about narrowing in on some special phrase or other.

**Step 3: Make adjustments**

The work Thea is doing is not unlike the work Clara did—it's just on a deeper and more fundamental level. The final step is to start gently challenging and reworking these beliefs. Core beliefs wouldn't be such a problem if they were broadly positive, life-affirming, rational, and based in reality. But let's be honest, most of them aren't!

The final stage of this process is far, far easier said than done. It is not enough to simply identify a better core belief and replace it—it will feel as difficult and unnatural to do as changing your name or even starting to think of yourself as a different race or nationality. It will take time, so be patient. Intellectually understanding that there is a better core belief out there ("I have intrinsic value just by being me") is not the same as feeling it. Remember, a core belief is not a string of words, it's a feeling.

So how do you change that core feeling that's at the heart of your entire life?

The answer is slowly. Every time you challenge the core belief, you weaken it. Every time you deliberately look for evidence for an alternative, you build up momentum for a different way of thinking—and feeling. Every time you give yourself the opportunity to behave differently and to achieve different results, you gradually loosen the grip of the old mentality and replace it with something else.

It's important to emphasize, again, that simply knowing what the better belief is won't be enough. You need to practice it. To really feel it. Remember that you only hold on to core beliefs because you've told yourself that story many, many times. Saying something different once or twice is not going to suddenly turn things around. In Thea's case, she decides that she wants to shift her core belief to reflect the *feeling* of being good enough just as she is. How can she do this?

Here are a few ideas:

- Every time she notices that core belief pop up, she argues with it. She deliberately tells herself the opposite. "No, Thea, you don't have to earn anything! You have value. Right now, without doing anything." She might not always believe it, but at least the same old story is not going unchallenged.
- She creates opportunities for herself to feel that good-enough-as-I-am feeling. For example, she spends time

with people she knows love her for who she is and not what she can or has achieved. She pauses to let this feeling really sink in and change her on a deep level.

- She looks back retroactively to find evidence for her alternative belief. She looks at pictures of herself as a child to remind herself of how she was perfectly lovable and valuable even though she hadn't earned any accolades and didn't have an impressive resume.
- She acts as though the alternative core belief were true, then adjusts to accommodate the outcome. If you believed fundamentally in your own innate worth, how would you act? Thea notices that she often belittles herself in company and puts herself down for being older and retired. But she realizes that if she believed in her value, she wouldn't do this. She would instead be proud of her achievements, secure in herself, and carry her head high. So this is what she does. To her surprise, she starts to notice that this gradually shifts her perception and how she feels.

You might have noticed the overlap between values and core beliefs. Values can be understood as conscious and positive—they are the guiding principles around which we wish to shape our lives. Core beliefs, however, especially if they're harmful or negative, are unconscious. They also shape our lives, but in hidden and seldom positive ways. Identifying your values can give you a yardstick against which to compare the core beliefs that you *actually* hold. So, in Thea's case, it is as though she has been living under the core "values" of lack of worth. What she is doing with the above, however, is restructuring her life so that it reflects a new value—the value of dignity, self-esteem, pride, and so on.

What are your core beliefs? Be patient, have self-compassion, and have a genuine curiosity about those assumptions you hold most dear. It's not important where these beliefs come from. They could be from early (or not so early) life experiences, from your upbringing, from a traumatic experience, from the culture around you . . . or you may never know why they happen at all. What's important is that with honest *awareness*, you have a say whether you want to keep believing in that assumption—or whether you're ready to try imagining a different way of living.

## Part 4: Opposite Action

Your brain has evolved over tens of thousands of years to help you survive, learn, adapt, and thrive in a complex and changing environment. What about your emotions—what is their purpose? Well, it's the same. Emotions can protect us, guide us, and help us survive just as surely as our problem-solving capacity and ability to be creative.

That's probably why most people now believe that suppressing your emotions is a bad idea—aren't you supposed to feel what you feel, express it, own it? Well, yes and no. That's because not all emotions are created equal. Remember Clara? Her cognitive power was both useful and harmful—it was her job to discern the difference and make conscious choices. It's the same with emotions. While it's true that it is never wrong to feel how we feel, it's also true that too much emotion can be debilitating and work against us.

Enter the technique of "opposite action." This technique is practiced in dialectical behavioral therapy (DBT), which was first developed by psychologist Marsha Linehan in the 1980s. **The goal was not emotional *suppression* but emotional *regulation*.**

Unfortunately, modern life teaches us to block out or avoid our emotions. Most of us have a very distorted idea of what it means to "regulate" our emotions. Alcohol, drugs, and workaholism all help us avoid our emotions. The "tricks" our bodies use to constrain our emotional awareness (e.g., holding the breath, muscle tension) only exacerbate anxiety, sadness, or physical difficulties (e.g., migraines or digestive problems).

According to DBT, every emotion has an action impulse. When we're afraid, we may want to flee the source of our uneasiness. With melancholy, we may retreat, isolate ourselves, or become passive. When furious, we may become defensive or attack. When practicing opposite action, we notice the emotion and action impulse. Then we do the opposite. Basically, we behave in a way that opposes the emotional impulse in order to dampen or downregulate our mood.

This idea may contradict your presumption of how to dispel an unpleasant mood. It was once believed that engaging in a great deal of emotional expression would reduce powerful feelings through "catharsis." For instance, you may have heard that it's helpful for an angry person to hit a punching bag and "blow off steam." However, recent psychological research has shown that this actually *intensifies* the emotion. The more you engage in an activity that is motivated by emotion, the more that behavior fuels your emotions.

Thankfully, the opposite is also true. **The more you participate in counter-emotional conduct (not *anti*-emotional conduct!), the less influence these strong negative emotions have on you.**

**Steps to Regulate Your Emotions**

**Step 1: Ask whether a strong emotion is actually working for you**

There's nothing wrong with emotion per se, and there isn't even anything wrong with strong emotion. Without it, life would be pretty pointless, right? So, it's not about which emotions are "negative" or which are "too strong," but more about whether your internal emotional experience is actually something you want, and whether it's helping or hindering you.

A tool that can help you identify your emotions is the Emotion Wheel. You can also consult online lists of emotion words to help you put a finger on exactly what you're feeling—which is a valuable exercise in itself!

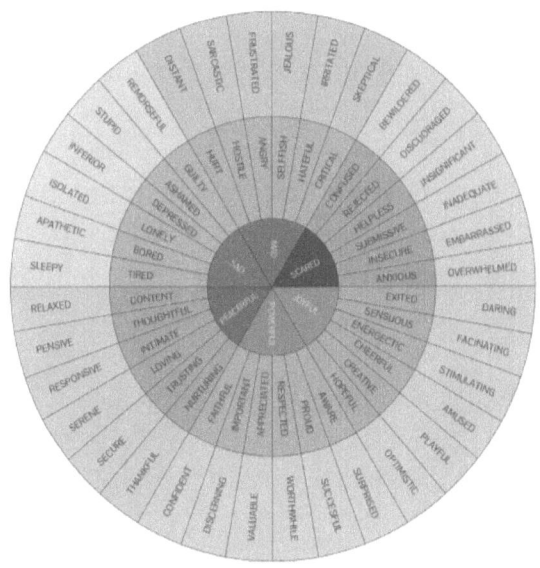

Once you've identified the emotion, ask what its consequences are. What thoughts and behaviors accompany it? Are these thoughts and actions in line with your values or your stated goals? Do you *like* how it's playing out?

**Step 2: Identify the urge that comes with your emotion**

All emotions have evolved for a purpose—they inspire or inhibit actions. How does your emotion make you want to act? Here is a quick list of some of the urges that are associated with different feelings.

- Anger: Aggressively engaging or attacking

- Disgust: Avoiding or pushing away

- Sadness: Withdrawing from activity and disengaging from people

- Fear: Avoiding or escaping

- Joy: Engaging with people and engaging in activity

Note that you don't necessarily have to have engaged in this way—only that you feel compelled to. Note also that the impulse or the action can range from small to large, strong to weak. There may be more than one impulse, too.

## Step 3: Engage fully in the exact opposite behavior of the emotional urge

Do this until you feel that the emotion has significantly lessened in intensity. Did you notice something? You are not trying to force the opposite *emotion*—but trying out the opposite *action*. Denying and suppressing emotion is not really possible or recommended. But if you change the way you're acting, you may find that it's far easier to manage and moderate emotions.

So, for example, if you're angry, your impulse might be to attack. What's the opposite action to attacking? Retreating. So, you could take a short break, excuse yourself from a stressful conversation, go take a walk on your own to cool off, or have a long, vigorous workout to dissipate all that energy in a harmless direction.

If you're disgusted, you might want to retreat, but instead, try to approach the thing with curiosity. Instead of physically wincing and tensing your muscles, engage with the stimulus while consciously relaxing your body. If you're depressed, your tendency might be to hide in a hovel and do nothing (like Nick!), but push yourself to do the opposite—go out and be active, meet people, connect, and do things—yes, even if you don't feel like it.

**Remember that you are not trying to force a particular emotion; you are only consciously choosing an *action*.** If you must, tell yourself you can feel whatever you like—as long as you still act in the way you chose. Have you ever noticed that you seem to be having a good time even though you were only a moment ago committed to being grumpy and in a bad mood? You won't believe it at first, sure, but simply acting in a less depressed way may be what you need to fake it till you make it.

Don't worry if things feel fake at first. Try to do the opposite action for a little while—you can always revert back to another behavior if you really want. But make a deal with yourself that you will note the effects that opposite action has—is the original impulse still as strong? How do you feel now?

Let's look at an example. Jamie has what he suspects is a case of bipolar disorder, but his official psychiatric diagnosis is not important here. What is important is that Jamie often feels that he is at the mercy of his emotions and that they control his entire life. He goes through cycles where he is intensely motivated and excited by something new, only to find within a few weeks that objectively minor disappointments and setbacks have completely thrown him into despair, and then he is depressed, angry, irritated. Jamie is a passionate person, a deep thinker, sensitive, creative, and astute.

His emotions are not *wrong*. But on the other hand, Jamie is seldom calm, content, satisfied, relaxed, or comfortable, and he would also like to occasionally feel at peace, or just neutral. He would be if he was more in control of how his emotions were expressed, when, and for how long. Here's how he may begin to use the technique of opposite action to take back some control and awareness.

Let's say Jamie is approached by some interesting investors who want to work with him and help him launch his relatively successful business into entirely new domains. It's an exciting proposition, and Jamie is indeed so excited that he doesn't sleep properly for days. He becomes obsessed with the idea, feverishly making business plans and visualizing in vivid detail what his ultra-rich and successful future is going to look like. He is what psychologists would call manic.

He becomes aware of this happening and stops. He brings out a journal and slows down his thoughts. For a few minutes, he simply writes down how he is feeling, without judgment. He then takes a look at the page and consults an Emotion Wheel to identify the kinds of emotions he's experiencing and their intensity. Simply pausing this way and calling out the names of his emotions already give him a feeling of psychological distance and a degree of neutrality and control.

He notices he is feeling invigorated, brave, excited, daring, optimistic, invincible, even euphoric.

He then becomes curious about the effect these emotions are having on his life. What are the consequences? Well, he isn't sleeping, for one, and that's affecting his health. Come to think of it, he isn't eating properly, either. When he pauses to notice it, there are a lot of things he has neglected by hyper-focusing on his promising new obsession: his physical fitness, his ordinary day job, his family commitments.

He asks what kind of thoughts and actions result from these feelings and takes a few moments to write these thoughts down.

"This is your big break; it's all happening now."

"You're a genius."

"Other people have no idea how big this is going to be."

"Nothing matters more than this right now; this is *it*."

Now, some people might say such vaulting confidence and self-assuredness is a good thing. But there are no good or bad emotions. In DBT therapy, we are only interested in better understanding *what* these emotions are and *how* they play out—no value judgment needed. After journaling for some time, Jamie realizes that although he is feeling ultra-excited and fired up, these "good" emotions are actually wreaking havoc on his life.

He realizes that the way he is behaving doesn't actually align with his values. He sees a pattern. Because he tells himself, "Nothing matters more than this right now," he gives himself permission to neglect everything else in his life. Then two things happen. First, the Big Plan falls apart (or, more realistically, is just a little less dazzling than it seemed at first), and then Jamie is crushed and depressed. Next, once he comes back down to earth, Jamie realizes that the rest of his life is in shambles because of the choices he made while chasing his latest obsession.

So, this thought is a *direct cause* of feeling disappointed and depression and of certain concrete actions that undermine other important things in his life (for example, ignoring his girlfriend for a week straight). Emotions are neither good nor bad, but they can be useful or harmful—and if they get in the way of what matters, they're definitely harmful no matter how good they feel in the moment or how rational or inevitable they seem at the time.

Some self-regulation is required.

Once Jamie has identified his emotions, he asks what impulses they lead to. He notes down in his journal that these feelings make him want to

*Take a big risk.*

*Talk . . . a lot.*

*Start a dozen new sub projects and ideas.*

*Spend money indiscriminately.*

*Completely dismiss potential problems, hazards, and drawbacks.*

He knows that this behavior isn't working for him. In fact, all of the above eventually lead, one way or another, to him crashing and burning into a depression a few weeks or months later. He doesn't like *that*, either. What's the opposite of the above?

*Be cautious and careful with risk.*

*Hold your tongue; listen.*

*Pick one project that matters most, or simply pause and reevaluate rather than jumping into something new.*

*Save money.*

*Take into consideration hazards, drawbacks, and potential problems.*

One day Jamie wakes up to an exciting email from one of the new investors. They want him to meet a colleague of theirs who is an expert in a related field and is very keen to meet Jamie. The email is full of glowing praise and tempting offers. Jamie feels himself getting excited. He sees himself getting drawn into that strong emotional pull again (see why awareness is so important?). But he pauses. He looks at how he feels. He remembers his journaling work and decides to do the opposite.

He takes his time composing a thoughtful but not over-the-top email. He dedicates a few hours to researching the viability of certain proposed ideas rather than immediately shopping for luxury yachts in his head. He tells himself he's not spending any extra money for the next week or two. He asks questions and listens carefully to the answers he's given. And within a few hours, he actually notices that he feels different. Calmer. More balanced.

A few weeks later, something interesting happens: Jamie begins to realize that the new investors are nothing but hot air, and that by moderating and regulating his emotions, he dodged a bullet and avoided getting embroiled in what could have been a costly and embarrassing mistake on his part. We'll end Jamie's story by restating that **emotions are value neutral—it is up to us, our values, and our goals to determine whether an emotion is working or not**. Then we can take responsibility to manage that emotion. So, for one person, a little of Jamie's mega-confidence would be the direction to go, and caution and risk-aversion are the thing to avoid; for Jamie, it's the other way around!

**Summary**:

- Many mental health problems come down to a **lack of awareness** of our own thoughts, feelings, and core beliefs. Being your own therapist requires the willingness to be honest, ask questions,

and courageously take action according to the insights you glean.
- In CBT, we understand that not all thoughts are for our benefit, and that thoughts, feelings, and actions are all connected. What has been learned can be unlearned, and we can take automatic, negative, unhelpful, and unconscious thoughts and deliberately transform them into conscious, helpful ones that allow us to live the kind of lives we want to live.
- Using cognitive restructuring, we can rewrite or replace cognitive distortions, such as black-or-white thinking, catastrophizing, personalization, or mindreading. We become aware, we appraise the accuracy and usefulness of a thought, and then we rewrite it.
- The behavioral activation theory approaches the problem on the behavioral level, telling us we need to act to feel better instead of waiting until we feel better to act. Monitor your routine, get in touch with your values and goals, then schedule activities that make you feel good, adjust and reappraising as you go.
- Core beliefs are deeply held ideas that influence how we behave, our self-

identity, and our attitudes. Using the downward arrow technique, we keep asking questions to uncover our core beliefs, which can be changed.
- With the technique of opposite action, we engage fully in the exact opposite behavior of our initial emotional urge, and thus develop emotional regulation.

## Chapter 2: Understanding What You're Made Of

**Part 1: Self-Questioning**

What would it look like if you could be your own therapist?

This is not a hypothetical question. Literally imagine it now—how would you talk to yourself if you were responsible for providing your own mental health care?

Maybe you think that **a really good counselor or psychologist is extra caring and compassionate, non-judgmental, non-directive, wise, and mature**. Well, the good news is that if you want to, you can provide all these things for yourself without a stitch of formal training.

There's something else, however, that therapists are really good at, and it's how we began this chapter: asking questions. A therapist doesn't **tell** you what you are feeling, what's wrong with you, or how to solve your problems. Instead, they are curious. They **ask** what you are feeling, ask you to look at how you are functioning, and point you toward your own inner resources so you can start to solve your problems yourself. Why do they do this? Because they know that your life gets better *when you are more aware*. Telling somebody something doesn't increase their awareness. Asking them a question does.

**If you want to become your own therapist, you need to get good at asking yourself the right kind of question.** The "right kind" means those questions that create more awareness and shed light on new solutions, unconscious material, possibilities, and alternatives.

Self-questioning is a way to peek outside of the current boundaries and limitations of the problem we're experiencing. It's a way to find insight. What's important here is that when you ask this kind of question, you are not doing so in order to find the correct answer. You are doing so because the *process* of thinking about the answer is what provides insight . . . and gets you to step outside the box of your current predicament.

Ask yourself the right questions and you can

- Educate yourself about your problem
- Clarify what you want to achieve
- Assess your thoughts, beliefs, feelings, and behaviors
- Gain insight into recurring patterns
- See solutions and new alternatives
- Find forgiveness, understanding, and compassion for your present position

We can ask questions about our thoughts, our feelings, and our behaviors. We can ask them about the past, the future, or the present. We can ask fantastical hypothetical questions, or real, concrete ones. We can ask whatever we like—there are no limits. In a therapy session, a counselor will use questions like a flashlight, shining a beam of awareness onto areas of your life that you may not have looked too closely at before.

Here are a few common ones:

- What am I feeling now?
- What am I thinking now?

- In general, what do I think and feel in this situation?
- When are the times when I feel better, stronger, clearer, more capable?
- What is one thing (no matter how small) that I can change right now?
- What am I avoiding right now?
- If my friend was going through the same struggle as I am, how would I make sense of their situation? What would I say to them?
- Are my thoughts distorted in any way?
- Do I have any evidence for my assumptions?
- What am I actually afraid of here?
- How would I behave right now if I were the best version of myself?
- How am I making sense of my situation?
- If the worst thing happened, would it really be the end of the world (you may recognize these from an earlier chapter!)
- Are there any unproven assumptions I'm making right now?
- Have I felt this way before? What helped back then? What didn't?
- What core belief is activated right now?

- Will any of this matter in one year's time? In ten years?
- What are my values?
- What do I ultimately want to achieve?

Before we continue, though, a word of warning: **Just asking a question is not the same as self-therapy, and it's not the same as actually doing something about your problem.** A question can shed light on an issue, but that's all. It's *still* your job to take action inspired by what you learn. The above questions may be more or less useful for you, but it all depends on your unique situation. A therapist will know the right question to ask at the right time. But if we are our own therapists, we need to pay close attention and make sure we're not getting carried away with meaningless analysis that doesn't go anywhere.

One tip: avoid asking *why*. This seems like a reasonable thing to ask, but it actually doesn't provide any insight, only the illusion of insight. Such a question might keep you trapped within a certain perceptual box rather than showing you a way out of that box. Look at the following conversation Clara could potentially have with herself as her own therapist:

Why are you so anxious about everything all the time?

*I don't know. Maybe it's my mother. She was always like that. Maybe I learned it from her.*

Why?

*I think I always wanted her approval or something. I think I wanted to be like her in many ways, so I unconsciously mimicked her.*

Why did you want to be like her?

*I think I grew up in that generation where little girls were kind of expected to be just like their mothers. And I actually did admire her in many ways. But I also think that there's a cultural expectation for women to be quite neurotic at times, you know? All the women around me were a bit like that.*

Why?

*I'm not sure. It's probably a social conditioning thing. Then again, it could be genes...*

Asking why seldom yields genuine insight. Why? Jokes aside, it's because you don't know the answer! For Clara, it's not really important where her anxiety comes from or who's to blame. She could write the above kind of material in a journal for an hour every day and still be no closer to being less anxious in everyday life. If you lack insight, chewing over the same bits of information over and over again will not magically create fresh insight. You will simply reinforce all the same old assumptions, coming to faulty conclusions or going round in circles.

What matters is what is happening, how, and when. What matters is her scope of action to choose to do something different. It's useless to try to guess reasons (none of which can be proven or disproven, by the way), but it *will* be useful for Clara to get clear on what she wants and what concrete action she can take right now to bring her closer to that.

Be careful about churning psychological material round and round in your own head and convincing yourself that this somehow equates to making change, learning about yourself, or solving problems. As you can see in the conversation above, nothing new is learned, and no shift in perception is achieved. The only thing such a dialogue can achieve is creating the illusion that you know yourself very well and are keenly on top of your own issue—while at the same time being as ignorant as ever and doing precisely zero to change the conditions of your life in real terms!

## The Miracle Question

No matter what predicament you are currently facing, there is one particular question that has been shown to be pretty helpful in creating insight. Does the "miracle question make miracles"? In therapy, it does. For the therapist, the intervention can help find clients' hidden strengths as well as new solutions to their problems (Yu, 2019). The miracle question opens doors to new possibilities because it essentially asks you to **imagine what things would be like if things were different**, better, and problems were solved (Strong & Pyle, 2009). This is a powerful question to ask because it focuses your mind not on the problem or on what isn't working, but on solutions, potentials, and options.

In solution-focused therapy, the client imagines and talks about a world where all the current problems don't exist and every issue is already dealt with. What does that look like? Just imagining it can help unlock ideas that were previously hidden by a focus on the lack or difficulty in the present.

The question can be asked in different ways:

- "Assume your problem has been solved. What has changed?"
- "Assume your problem is gone. What does this mean to you?" (Strong & Pyle, 2009, p. 334).
- "Suppose tonight, while you are asleep, a miracle happens. Because you were asleep, you didn't know it had happened, but everything you ever wanted is now there, and all your problems are gone. You now have your perfect life. When you wake in the morning, **how will you be able to tell that the miracle has happened**?"

This last bit is important. How will you be able to tell that the miracle has occurred? What will you see? Hear? Touch? What kind of a person will you be? What are your thoughts, feelings, actions? What would your world have to look like for you to wake up and encounter it in the morning and exclaim "it's a miracle"? What would other people see and notice for them to think the same thing?

When you ask this question, really give yourself the time to answer it fully. Close your eyes and immerse yourself in a possible answer. Don't jump in with "yes, but . . ." or reasons for why the miracle can't happen. Just assume it *did*, no matter how unlikely or crazy that seems to you right now. Become curious about what you notice after this miracle has completely come and gone. Be creative! If you can, spend up to ten minutes doing this exercise and dwell on each detail. Then what? Remember that we are not just asking questions for nothing. Our insight only counts if we channel it into useful, value-driven, goal-oriented behavior that makes our lives better. Let's look at how that could happen.

Let's say Clara asks herself the Miracle Question and fleshes out a full answer. Clara is an anxious overthinker who can't help catastrophizing and assuming the worst outcome on zero evidence. Her core belief, if you remember, is something like, "The world can't be trusted and I am not safe." She knows that she is anxious. She imagines that one day, she wakes up and a miracle has occurred. How would she know?

She imagines herself relaxed, joyful, balanced. She really feels into this sensation of calm control, of feeling *trust* in herself and the world at large. It's quite a luxurious feeling! She knows a miracle has happened because when she encounters a stressful trigger, she doesn't care. It means nothing to her. In fact, she finds herself exploring all kinds of interesting new possibilities in this miracle world. If she truly miraculously felt safe in life, would she stay at her job? Stay with her boring but stable husband? She follows the visualization wherever it takes her. She would travel. She would try new things and take more risks. She'd dress more creatively, take up painting, and be less afraid of speaking her mind in conversations. If she truly felt safe in herself and in the world, she realizes, she'd suddenly feel creative, inspired, curious . . . how different life would look!

Once she opens her eyes, it's time to put this understanding into practice. Clara now goes about her normal life again, but the next time she faces a stressful trigger or notices herself going into catastrophizing mode, she stops and asks, "How would I behave if the miracle had happened?" Then she does that. That's important—she needs to **act**, not just imagine.

She's scrolling on her phone (kryptonite for anxious overthinkers!) and stumbles upon a panic-inducing news report about nuclear war. She can't help the automatic thought that pops into her mind: "The whole thing is hopeless. Sooner or later, humans are going to blow themselves to smithereens, and there's nothing you can do about it!" She looks at this thought and imagines how she would appraise it if the miracle had happened.

Well, she would feel a moment of stress, but then realize that there really isn't anything she can do, and that stressing about it won't change a thing. So why voluntarily stress? If she had trust in herself (and perhaps even in a higher power), she would put away her phone and decide to be grateful for her life, to live right now, and to refuse to be guided by fear. If she wanted to, she could take conscious action that would work to reinforce her values, like donating to a refugee support program. Or maybe she'd go into the other room, hug her husband, and then carry on with creating the life she actually wants—like putting in a few hours of practice painting!

Every morning, Clara reminds herself of the miracle question and how it felt to be outside of her current problem of anxiety. Remember, it's not only a verbal or intellectual exercise—she is trying not only to think something different, but to really *feel* it. Every evening, she looks at how her thoughts, feelings, and behaviors have changed. It will sound cheesy, but one day, Clara will wake up and *she will be living that miracle*. The exercise will seem boring to her because she is no longer imagining anything. It's real.

## Part 2: Delving into the Shadows

When most people experience uncomfortable emotions, they want to do one thing and one thing only: get away from them. In fact, you may have picked up this very book with the unconscious expectation that it would relieve you from having to experience unpleasant feelings, and take all of that away.

However, this is the opposite of the mindset you need. As we saw above, what's required is a willingness to tolerate, accept, and be with emotions, **all our emotions**, no matter how uncomfortable they are, and without judgment.

If you start to make awareness and self-exploration a bigger part of your life, sooner or later, you're going to encounter parts of yourself that you really, really don't like. Self-therapy contains a kind of irony—the process of improvement tends to bring *more* awareness to what isn't working, not less. However, our goal is not simply to numb ourselves or pretend away unpleasant truths. It's to genuinely improve, grow, and heal. This is where the technique of shadow work comes into play.

Carl Jung was the psychiatrist, author, and theorist who first introduced the idea of the shadow. In simple terms, the shadow is our psychological blind spot—it contains everything that we can't "see"—i.e., that is outside our awareness. Every person has a shadow, but the idea is that if we can acknowledge it, accept it, and integrate it back into our awareness as something that rightly belongs to us, we enjoy greater mental health, authenticity, creativity, energy, and maturity. If you engage in self-therapy to any degree, you *will* bump up against the shadow at some point. How you deal with it makes all the difference in the world.

When we are young, we have certain experiences that teach us that some parts of ourselves are acceptable and others aren't. In order to survive in the world and get our needs met, we unconsciously decide to disown those "bad" parts of ourselves and disidentify with them. We push them out of awareness.

For example, our parents may tell us that our anger is bad and punish us when we yell or express frustration. So, we put "anger" into the shadow. It hasn't gone anywhere, but we don't see it anymore.

This "dark side" of our conscious awareness doesn't contain just bad things, by the way. We can also disconnect from and disown positive feelings, attributes, or thoughts. We may put into the shadow things like excitement, hope, silliness, and so on because of early experiences that taught us these things were bad.

So what's the problem? Isn't it a good thing to section off the worst parts of ourselves? The trouble is that the shadow is never completely hidden. It still shows itself; however, it may do so in sneaky ways. Our shadow may express itself in strange behaviors we don't understand—in dreams, in slips of the tongue, or in behavior others can see but we don't ourselves recognize.

Perhaps our anger comes out in passive aggressiveness. We may say, "I'm the least angry person in the world!" Yet somehow, others can *feel* the anger radiating off us anyway. It's because it's still there, in the shadow. As long as we have a shadow, we will remain at least partly unconscious of our deeper motivations and may be trapped in behaviors that are not good for us, without really understanding why.

On top of this, there's a sneaky phenomenon called projection, in which we end up incorrectly ascribing to others the feelings and thoughts we ourselves have but have disowned and relegated to the shadow. The classic example is the person who is being dishonest but has pushed that fact out of awareness. The shadow seeps out, however, in the form of them constantly accusing *others* of hiding something or being dishonest. They're projecting when they say, "The problem isn't in me; it's in you!"

In this way, what we are unconscious of can harm us. It can threaten our relationships, jeopardize our work, and weaken our potential. It can also leave us confused, immature, and fragile people who lack wisdom and self-knowledge. The solution? Again, it's awareness! According to Jung, **we improve our lives and heal when we integrate the shadow.**

That may sound like a good idea, but nobody wants to look at their shadow. Nobody wants to face up to the things they cannot face in themselves, by definition! So how exactly do we see what we can't see? Let's explore a few fundamental techniques and look at how Nick (who you'll remember from a previous chapter) can apply them to his life. Recall that Nick is battling a lack of motivation, depression, procrastination, and an overall pessimistic and passive attitude to life. What do you think is in *his* shadow?

**Accepting the Shadow**

Before going any further, be aware that what you *don't* want to do is continue to judge and condemn the "bad" parts of yourself—after all, this is precisely what caused it to be shoved out of awareness in the first place. No, we cannot be whole and integrate the shadow by heaping on more scorn or shame. Instead, we need to be curious, compassionate, and open-minded.

To engage our shadow, we need a few things:

- Patience
- A genuinely accepting and nonjudgmental attitude
- Honesty
- The willingness to be brave enough to face things we don't like about ourselves

Here are a few ways to do that.

**Technique 1: Pay attention to your emotional reactions**

Imagine someone has a drinking problem that they can't quite admit to themselves. In their shadow is everything they deny about themselves: a lack of self-control, frequent reckless behavior, even the habit of denial itself. They are unwilling to face up to the fact that they behave in ways they don't like when they drink too much, and are unwilling to accept the shame they feel because of it. In fact, they could go for years never acknowledging this problem.

One day, this person notices themselves feeling extremely judgmental about a friend who smokes marijuana. They say, "It's totally irresponsible. Don't they care about what they're doing to their health? So reckless. They obviously lack self-control! I'm so disappointed in them . . ." Others might be puzzled at this outburst. Why such a strong reaction?

The answer probably lies in the person's shadow. Read through their thoughts again, and you'll see that this is in fact what they think of *themselves*. The shadow can hide from awareness, but it often shows itself as judgment of others, or strong and disproportionate reactions that don't quite fit the situation at hand.

In Nick's case, one day he hears about an old friend from middle school who he hasn't seen in years. He's told that this friend has made a real success of his life and is now happily married with a thriving business and two gorgeous kids. Nick hears this story and instantly finds himself angry and annoyed. He finds himself making snide comments about how this friend probably just got lucky. He dwells on the idea, mocking and dismissing this friend's success, even accusing him of being a fake or a sellout. When someone teases Nick and suggests that maybe he's just jealous, Nick blows up. "Jealous? Of *that* idiot? No thanks. At least I'm not some corporate moron who's happy to sell his soul. In fact, I pity him!"

Can you see what's happened? In Nick's shadow is everything that he sees as not a part of him—that means self-esteem, pride, and success. This friend sets Nick off because he reminds him of this disowned part of Nick who would prefer to think of himself as powerless and a bit of a victim. Imagine that what Nick says about this friend is actually what he himself is saying to that part of his psyche that represents competence, success, pride, and mastery. His violent reaction to these things in someone else is evidence of just how unable he is to accept them in himself. In Nick's case, integrating the shadow would mean acknowledging that if the friend can do it, so can he. It would mean reconnecting with his own feelings of pride and success and admitting that living an impressive life is something that he does, in fact, want.

It's a good idea to become aware of anything that seems to "push your buttons" and cause a reaction that is bigger than it should be. Prick your ears if you seem to have been "triggered" automatically by something, and become curious why. What bothers you in others is often something you've disowned in yourself!

**Technique 2: Embrace imperfection**

While rage, jealousy, and lust are all understandably relegated to the shadow, much of what we put there isn't really so bad when you think about it. The shadow may feel big and scary and overwhelming, but it's often like the monster under the bed—when you peek to check, there's nothing there.

If you can learn to embrace flaws and imperfection and accept that **you are a**

**complex person with both good and bad qualities**, then you weaken the power of the shadow. One way to do this is to consciously decide you will judge and condemn others less often (hint: to the extent you judge them, you also judge yourself). Another idea is to deliberately ask, "What's so wrong with being a flawed human being?"

Here's an exercise to try.

> 1. Identify the attributes, ideas, thoughts, or feelings you most often judge in others.
> 2. Write them down ("I hate stupid people").
> 3. Now rephrase the sentences so they apply to you ("I can be stupid sometimes").
> 4. Read through these new sentences and notice how you feel. Ask yourself, is it *really* the end of the world if they're true? Does it mean that you're not worthy of love, or that you don't also possess good qualities? You may notice that the more forgiving you are about other people's stupid mistakes, the easier it is to accept occasional stupidity in yourself, and vice versa.

5. If you're having trouble, try to imagine a loved one who has that attribute, yet whom you still adore and respect anyway (maybe you realize that your pet Labrador is the stupidest being on the planet, but that doesn't stop them from also being the one you love most!). Imagine that you, too, are perfectly acceptable as you are, warts and all.

## Technique 3: Ask for feedback

Your shadow is a bit like the back of your head—you can't see it, but it may be very visible to everyone else!

Asking someone you trust and respect to help you see your blind spots takes some courage, but it's well worth it. Identify someone you believe knows you well—the last thing you want is to ask someone who will accidentally project their own shadow onto you! Ask someone who themselves has been able to demonstrate emotional maturity, and who will be happy to help you look objectively at your shadow without bringing judgment into the equation.

Since this may be a tall order, another option is to enlist the help of a therapist, counselor, or psychologist to help you work through the more sensitive parts of your shadow. They'll be able to hold you accountable while keeping a "safe space" that won't trigger more defensiveness in you.

If both of these options are not feasible, you can always sit down and carefully consider the feedback you've already received from others. Can you find any themes or patterns in what you've been told by ex-partners, old bosses (or current ones!), friends, family members, or even random people? You may already have been given heaps of feedback that consistently points to your shadow, only you haven't been courageous enough to take it fully on board.

Notice if you repeatedly find yourself angry with people's appraisals of who you are (again, it's about noticing *disproportionate* reactions) and ask honestly if they may have a point. Think back to disagreements you may have had or recall criticisms or advice others may have repeatedly given you. You may have dismissed it in the past, but could it be that others have said similar things? Could there be a pattern?

The important thing about shadow work is that you are not trying to play "gotcha"! You are not attempting to catch yourself out or punish yourself. If on reflection you notice that more than a handful of people have mentioned how over the top you can be at times, just own and acknowledge that. Avoid getting lost in shame or embarrassment about it—just accept it gracefully and be proud of yourself that you're able to be aware.

If that fails, one technique always works: humor. Laugh at yourself a little. "Oh, there I go again! What a drama llama I am. How do you put up with me?"

"Shadow work is all about the unconscious mind," says Danielle Massi, LMFT. She says that your shadow self might come out when you're upset, in your relationships, or when you're feeling different levels of anxiety and depression. **Rather than trying to flee the shadow when it rears its head, though, try to see it as an opportunity to learn something interesting about who you are**. The next time a "negative" emotion arises in you, pause, become aware, and become curious about what it might say about your shadow.

## Part 3: Understanding Avoidance Mechanisms

At this point in our book, it's worth dwelling further on this idea of self-sabotage. As we saw in the last chapter, **our shadow, so long as it is unconscious, can and very often does undermine us and work against what we say we want for ourselves.** Remember Thea and her core belief that she only has worth if she is constantly providing something of value to others? Well, so long as she is unaware of this core belief, it will continue to sabotage her, all the while she is saying superficially, "I have high self-confidence. I love who I am. I started my own business, I've received awards, and I'm considered an expert in my field—of course I don't have any issues with my own value!"

If Thea went to see a counselor and spoke this way, she may spend many sessions never really getting to the root of the issue. And if Thea embarked on her own mission to self-therapize but without ever addressing this major blind spot and lack of awareness, the result would be the same: Nothing would change. In fact, many people reach a point in their lives when they have so totally bought into their own avoidance mechanisms that they have almost convinced themselves there is no problem—almost. But late at night, when they're alone in bed, it all comes rushing back to them. They think: "What's wrong with me?"

What's "wrong" is that they've gotten really, really good at avoiding the problem!

So, before we carry on and explore more self-therapy techniques, let's commit to being as honest with ourselves as we can. It is not wrong to have a shadow or to want to protect oneself psychologically from the awareness of certain painful realities. But, unless we can start to consciously and compassionately grow our awareness anyway, we cannot hope to really grow or change. Certainly, we will just be wasting our time with various techniques and tricks since we'll engage with them only in superficial ways, carefully avoiding the one thing that actually needs attention.

Avoidance, denial, distraction—these are not always bad things. We can't be aware of all things at all times. Sometimes, it takes a while for us to work up the courage, maturity, and energy to face something head-on. In Thea's case, retirement was a major life stage and a big psychological transition—akin to puberty or becoming a parent. Because she was so unprepared for it, it took her a while to wake up to the problem. For a few months, she distracted herself with busy work that helped her avoid becoming aware of how she really felt. Every time the idea "I'm worthless now" vaguely edged into her awareness, she'd sign up for some course or class or undertake a drastic project that would take all her time.

This is normal! Just like puberty doesn't happen overnight, nor does a parent figure it all out in a week, Thea needed time to gather up awareness of what was happening in her world. All of this is to say that our goal is never to pounce on denial or avoidance in ourselves whenever we suspect it. Rather, we are always maintaining an attitude of gentle, non-directive curiosity and compassion. And it takes time. Saying "I mustn't think of that awful thing" is denial, but on the other hand, saying "I absolutely must face and confront this awful thing right now!" is not all that helpful, either.

**Simply ask instead, *"Is there something I'm avoiding right now? Why? Am I ready to be more honest and aware about some things?"***

An avoidance mechanism is a way to cope with difficulties. This is important—it is a legitimate way to cope. It's just not usually a very *effective* way to cope. When you identify denial and avoidance in yourself, the idea is not that you snatch that security blanket away, but rather that you become curious about *better ways* to cope.

There are many ways that people use avoidance to protect themselves, to manage strong emotions, to regulate, and to feel safe and in control.

- **Acting out** – behaving in destructive or distracting ways that express pain without really acknowledging it
- **Avoidance and denial** – simply not engaging with a threatening idea, thought, feeling, person, or place
- **Displacement** – shifting your action to a "safer" but unrelated target
- **Escaping into fantasy** – daydreams, wishful thinking, and playing with entertaining and hopeful possibilities

that draw awareness away from *what is*
- **Projection** – incorrectly ascribing to others the feelings and thoughts we ourselves have but have disowned and relegated to the shadow
**Intellectualization and rationalization** – avoiding emotion by retreating into words, logic, symbols, and safe abstractions
- **Trivializing and humor** – A threatening idea is less threatening if you pretend that it's small, silly, or laughable
- **Reaction formation** – Avoiding something by doing exactly the opposite, or deliberately adopting the counter perspective

There are many more forms of avoidance and defense, but as you can probably tell, each of the above is really a variation on a single theme. They all act to *reduce and limit awareness*. The precise way they do it is less important. What matters is that they all work to narrow perception, distort your perspective, and restrict the amount of information you are taking in from the world around you. This can work temporarily, but as we see in Thea's case, there comes a time when it stops working.

After a year or so of rushing around and trying to fill every spare moment of time so she doesn't have to feel uncomfortable feelings, she finds herself feeling restless. She notices her continued discomfort around those who are still working. For Thea, she is experiencing a kind of denial that keeps certain painful ideas firmly in the shadow. Her core belief ("I'm worthless unless I work") is unconscious. She can't acknowledge it. But what she *can* do is work. When she works, she feels like she has worth. So that's what she does.

Because avoidance mechanisms help you cope by restricting awareness, bringing awareness to them may feel (at first) like they make coping more difficult. That's why it's important to *replace* coping mechanisms, not eliminate them. But first . . .

**How Do I Possibly Know if I'm in Denial?**

It's tricky, isn't it?

All of us are likely in denial about something at some point in our lives. Perhaps we know, but we don't know we know! The signs that we are avoiding a problem are not dissimilar from the signs that we are touching upon some material from our shadow: disproportionate emotional responses, looking at the judgments we throw at others, and how we respond to what people around us are telling us. There are a few other clues that you may be avoiding something.

- You feel annoyed when asked to talk about the issue and can notice yourself just rushing through or past the topic as quickly as possible, or changing the topic altogether.
- You often catch yourself "explaining" your actions and choices to others, i.e., justifying things. It's a little like "the lady doth protest too much"—your very insistence on a lengthy justification often shows how flimsy it really is.
- There's a knee-jerk feeling of needing to blame someone or something else.
- You behave in ways that even you don't understand and can't explain. You may see the bad results of this behavior and yet can't seem to stop.
- You feel like you *know* something is a problem, but you'll get around to fixing it all later. You say things like, "I

know, I know," and brush off people's concern or advice, claiming you're already doing what needs to be done. Or will do it in the future. Maybe.
- You actively catch yourself pushing certain thoughts out of your mind. Have you ever said, "Well, there's no point talking/thinking about it"?

In real life, it's difficult to see what your mind doesn't want you to see, and, if people are honest, sometimes we gain deeper awareness of ourselves spontaneously, and not because we have been ultra-honest with ourselves and diligent in our personal development. We can face difficult things when we're ready to. That means one of our jobs is to make sure we're ready! We can do this by regarding ourselves with care and compassion, respecting our process even if it isn't perfect, and being patient as we learn and grow. It comes back to awareness.

**How to Look at a Blind Spot**

The avoidance coping mechanism switches on when we're faced with a threat—or the *perception* of a threat. But what would happen if we tolerated that threat instead? What if we maintained awareness and didn't attempt to flee that uncomfortable sensation?

Thea is in a café, and a waitress smiles at her and says, "Having a nice, relaxing day?" It's a meaningless comment, but Thea immediately starts to feel a vague sense of irritation. The waitress triggers all sorts of core beliefs and knee-jerk reactions in Thea. She begins to think, "What did she mean by that? Does she think I'm some kind of slob? Was it some kind of dig because I'm not at work?"

It might seem extreme, but be honest—haven't you experienced similar thought cascades after a seemingly innocent comment? They may simmer just below the surface of awareness, but nevertheless, the result is clear: It feels uncomfortable. Now, Thea has two choices. She can flee that discomfort, or she can tolerate it. Sit with it. Get to know it better. Importantly, it's not the situation she would be avoiding or facing, but the **discomfort**.

What happens to discomfort when you are comfortable with it?

Let's say Thea goes home, noticing that her mood has gone a little sour. She pauses and, instead of cheerily putting on a brave face, pretending she's fine, or blaming and displacing ("I'm fine. I just feel a little jumpy after too much coffee, that's all"), she admits how she feels. She owns and acknowledges it. Imagine now that she thinks of this discomfort as a person and pictures herself having a conversation with it.

"Hi, discomfort. What are you here for? What do you want to tell me?"

Then, she listens without judgment, shame, or blame. Instead of explaining away or arguing with the discomfort, she tries to understand it better. Many of us have been socialized to deny our fears, our angers, our irritations, our vulnerabilities. We don't want to admit to ourselves or others that we are having difficulty with something. But if Thea can begin to be honest about what she actually feels, then she can begin to admit other things to herself: "*I'm* the one who judges myself for relaxing. It's not the waitress's fault. I feel guilty when I'm not working." This leads to more and more awareness. Diving into the difficult feeling will, in the long run, lead to less of that feeling.

Discomfort is, well, uncomfortable. But if we engage with it and acknowledge it consciously, it offers a chance for us to actually move on, solve problems, find insight, and evolve. Thea could never start to work on her sabotaging core beliefs and begin to live a more authentic life until she is actually honest about what she feels and what is currently difficult.

This is a subtle point but a powerful one to master. In today's personal development and self-help world, "toxic positivity" is inadvertently teaching us to flee discomfort rather than tolerate it and see what it can teach us. We would rather *pretend* that we are happy and in control than face the uncomfortable reality that there are things we are afraid of, unsure of, or angry about. But it's these parts of our psyches that feel raw, embarrassing, scary, shameful, and unfinished that are actually the places where we find our greatest potential. All it takes to tap that potential is a willingness to bear with our discomfort. Think of it as deciding to clear away a big scary debt—you can't begin to plan ahead or fix the problem until you face it and see in crystal-clear detail what the outstanding figure is.

If you sense that secrets, denial, and avoidance are a big part of your life right now, vow that you will proceed from now on with equal parts curiosity and compassion. Ask yourself, "If I was not afraid, what would I be able to admit to myself right now?" Then, listen quietly and accept with kindness whatever bubbles up to the surface.

## Part 4: Gestalt Techniques—The Empty Chair

In the previous chapter, we saw how Thea adopted a completely different attitude to her own discomfort and avoidance. Instead of fleeing difficult emotions, she turned to face them and ask them questions, opening herself up to learning more about who she really was. In gestalt therapy, there is a technique called the "empty chair," which takes this principle to the extreme and asks practitioners to imagine themselves addressing another person, a feeling, an idea, or even a part of themselves as though it were sitting across from them in a chair.

So, Thea took her uneasy emotion and her sense of discomfort and made it a person, sat it down, and spoke to it. That emotion spoke back. In the dialogue, she learned something important—not to mention she finally took control of her situation rather than just reacting unconsciously. **In gestalt therapy,**

**what matters is the present.** The past can haunt us in the form of trauma, bad habits, old acquired assumptions, beliefs, and so on. But, when we pull all of that from out of the past and bring it to the present, **we give ourselves the chance to process it in the here and now, to "update," and to sincerely move on.**

Does it feel silly to do the empty chair technique? A little—but only at first. It can also be a very powerful way to heal, to grapple with grief, to gain insight into your own hangups, and to make a move toward real integration and wholeness. The process is simple (note—not easy!):

1. **Identify the topic or issue** that you're trying to work on or gain additional insight in. Imagine that Jamie, from previous examples, wants to gain some healing around his cycles of euphoria/depression.
2. **Take one seat for yourself and position an empty seat next to it.** Now, imagine that in this seat is a person related to the issue you've identified. This could be a real person you know or knew, someone from

the past, your childhood self, or even a potential person who might exist one day. It could be a personified emotion or your shadow itself. Let's say that after working on himself for some time, Jamie identifies a core belief: "I am falling behind in life. I need to catch up with everyone else." Perhaps he places this core belief or feeling in a chair. Perhaps he places his father in the chair, since this is the person who he associates this feeling most strongly with.

3. Next, take some time just to feel into the situation, **imagine the person in front of you in as much detail as you can**, and notice how you feel. Jamie notices a sinking, queasy feeling at the back of his throat, a tension, a deep sensation of panic and shame. He feels inadequate, but this feeling is heavily tinged with a sense of rushing and constantly running out of time or being evaluated.

4. **Now, *from that feeling*, speak to the person in front of you**.

Allow your emotion to speak. Express yourself directly, plainly, and as honestly as you can. As you do this, you might even spontaneously imagine that the person in the other chair responds—in that case, great, respond back! Have that dialogue. Get everything out there. For Jamie, speaking to his shame/father is a chance for him to admit (perhaps for the first time, even to himself) that he has always felt the pressure of needing to prove himself and perform, and that it's a crushing, constant fear that he wishes he could be rid of. That's why his bipolar experience has been one where he vacillates between grand plans where he'll finally strike it lucky, and deep depressions where he encounters how "far behind" he still is.

5. If you can, try to **complete the exercise by changing seats**—sit in the other chair and try to take on the perception and perspective of that other

person/idea. If you've put your shadow in the chair, for example, try to speak as it would speak. "I hate when you ignore me. I'm angry for a good reason, and when you pretend like I don't have a right to be angry, it makes me angrier!" For Jamie, speaking from the position of his own shame can be incredibly intense but healing. Doing so means he can understand why that shame is there and how it is trying to help him—indeed, that it is a part of him. Naturally, this step won't be appropriate for everyone and every situation, so use your discretion.

There are many variations on the empty chair technique, and lots of ways to make it work for you.

You could work your way through a tricky conflict you're having with someone by putting them on the seat (in your imagination, that is!). By speaking your peace but also seeing things through their eyes, you gain fresh insight into the issue, as well as some empathy for their situation.

This way, you can privately work out your own feelings and goals without getting embroiled in difficult conversations with others, or else you can use the technique to prepare for a potentially challenging conversation.

The technique is also used for "inner child work" where you are asked to both address and speak from the perspective of that part of you that is still childlike and innocent. A variation is to speak to yourself at a particular stage in your history, but take on a wiser, more caring, even adult perspective as you dialogue with this version of yourself. A common theme is to ask your younger self what they needed back then. How did they feel? Then, as the person you are now, you can take steps to provide that for yourself in the present. We'll be discussing this area of self-therapy in the next chapter.

One extremely useful way to use the empty chair is to speak to people you no longer can physically speak to—i.e., those who have passed. What do you wish you could still say to them? What do you need them to know? Working through things this way can be an enormous aid to letting go of and processing grief. Some people even find relief and meaning in talking to deceased ancestors and family members they never knew.

People who find it difficult to know and understand what they're feeling can use this technique when they want to get a firmer grasp on their own emotions. If your head is in a mess and you can't quite put words to how you're feeling, imagine that state of mind sitting in the seat. Explore it. Represent it to yourself in any way that makes sense—maybe it's a person, or maybe it's an animal, a symbol, a cartoon character, or some kind of mythical being. But the point is to give it a name, to externalize it so it's out there in the world, and to start engaging with it actively.

Your anxiety could be a giant egg threatening to crack. Your depression could be a black dog (like it was for Winston Churchill and the writer Samuel Johnson before him). Your secret yearning for greatness, pride, and vanity, on the other hand, could take the form of Winston Churchill draped with medals!

Jamie might practice this technique for a while, going deeper with it each time. Eventually, he may come to gain real insight into this *thing* that is making him feel inadequate so that he constantly needs to prove himself and achieve, and when he doesn't, he crashes in shameful disappointment. He gives this thing a name and an appearance—in his mind's eye, it is an old-school stock market broker who is angry and shouting, red in the face, and desperate to make that next big trade that's going to rocket him and everyone to mega-wealth.

Jamie sits down and has a productive conversation with this person—who is, after all, a part of him. He speaks with compassionate curiosity to the person (whom he's named Wolfie, inspired by the manic lead character in the movie *The Wolf of Wall Street*). He asks Wolfie, "How are you feeling?" and Wolfie explains that he *has* to make this next big deal work, or else. "Or else what?" asks Jamie. Wolfie mimes blowing his brains out with a pistol. "Why don't you just get a more normal job so you won't be so stressed all the time?" Jamie asks. "There's no time!" says Wolfie. "It's now or never."

Jamie could sit down with a therapist and talk endlessly about all-or-nothing cognitive distortions, about unrealistic expectations, about putting pressure on oneself, and about feeling driven to live up to parental expectations . . . but by using the empty chair technique, Jamie is learning to realize all this for himself. It may take some time, but such a technique works because it pulls up unconscious, automatic assumptions and habits and shows them in the light of consciousness. The next time Jamie feels like he's getting a little panicked, rushed, and manic, he reminds himself, "Oh, it's Wolfie speaking again. Hi, Wolfie! What brings you here?"

This technique teaches Jamie a few things:

- That his thoughts, reactions, feelings, and perceptions are not permanent and non-negotiable—they can change
- That he can always gain some psychological distance from whatever he is experiencing, and thus gain control
- That he need never be afraid of or ashamed of any part of himself—as long as he can talk to these different parts of his psyche with compassion and open-mindedness, what's the worst that could happen?

A few words of warning about this technique, however. **The process works best when you are open-minded and non-directive.** That means to not approach the problem forcefully and as though you have some pre-conceived idea of how you're going to fix the problem once and for all. Your goal should be more *receptive and exploratory.* Try it out, see what happens. Think of it in the same way you would meeting a completely new stranger. Just get to know them, ask questions, and see where it goes. Any fixed notions of how things "should" go is likely to tangle you up in knots fast.

You also don't have to give an Oscar-worthy performance, and the themes you explore don't have to "make sense." Just be real. Try not to expect some major catharsis or mind-blowing insight at the end, either (while it is possible, it's not the aim!).

Finally, remember that when it comes to self-therapy, what matters at the end of the day is concrete change. **Insight means nothing unless you actually allow it to be reflected in your life via action, choice, and behavior.** That's why you should end every empty chair session by exploring what you've learned and what it means moving forward. Self-questioning is important here, as is your conscious commitment to make different choices for yourself.

In Jamie's example, he learns to speak to Wolfie, telling him that he doesn't have anything to prove, that he can calm down, and that there's no rush to pull off any dazzling business feats of greatness or invent the next big thing. He writes this all down and repeats these mantras to himself throughout the day whenever he feels that creeping sense of panic and inadequacy. "Slow down," he tells himself. "That's Wolfie talking, and you don't have to listen."

In fact, after a while, Jamie decides to take this technique a little further. He sets out a chair for another character—this time, he invites his inner calm, stable, and rational self to take a seat and talk with him. At first, this character is not sure what to say (after all, it hasn't been listened to very much and is small and weak!), but in time, it grows. Sometimes he can imagine Wolfie arguing with this "higher self." Day to day, as Jamie explores this other, less-developed side of his own psyche, he notices that slowly, it is growing stronger. He doesn't allow negative self-talk to go unchallenged anymore. He still has moods and still experiences highs and lows, but his higher self is weighing in more often.

"Hey, Jamie, don't worry about all that. Wolfie is just afraid. Take a deep breath. You don't have to act right now. You're doing great. There is no competition, and you don't have to rush."

You might not have time for a full-blown empty chair session in everyday life, but take a page from Jamie's book, and when you find yourself feeling unhappy or anxious, ask your own higher self to check in and help you out. **What does the best version of you, your inner guru, have to say?** You may surprise yourself with just how wise it really is!

**Summary**:

- Self-therapy is about compassion but also about asking the right questions. The miracle question in particular asks us to imagine that the problem is already solved and to think about what that looks like. This helps us focus on solutions and possibilities. However, it's important to actually apply these insights and take appropriate action.
- Jung said the human "shadow" contains everything we don't accept in ourselves, but if we are able to tolerate all our emotions, we have a chance at wholeness

and integration of all aspects of ourselves. We can pay attention to disproportionate emotional responses, embrace our imperfection, and take feedback on board, all without shame or blame.
- Avoidance mechanisms can help protect us until we're ready to process difficult material, but we should get in the habit of asking ourselves if there is something we are deliberately avoiding becoming aware of. Signs of this are avoidance, projection, reaction formation, escapism, etc. Instead of fleeing discomfort, become curious about the function its fulfilling.
- Gestalt therapy's empty chair technique is about addressing a person, idea, or even part of the psyche as though it were sitting in an empty chair in front of you. This helps bring past patterns into the present so they can be processed. There are many variations, but all require an open, receptive mind and a non-directive attitude.

## Chapter 3: Where It All Came From

In Chapter 1, we asked about the thoughts, behaviors, and core beliefs that worked to shape and program our everyday responses to life. And in Chapter 2, we took a deeper look at how to self-question, how to explore our unconscious shadow, how to talk to and engage hidden parts of ourselves, and even how to gain new insight into our blind spots.

In this chapter, we'll explore yet another angle on which to approach the task of self-therapy—our childhoods—and how they impact our lives in the present. This cause-and-effect line of reasoning is an old principle that comes from the earliest psychodynamic therapists, but it remains a fundamental assumption: **If we want to know who we are now and why we are**

**that way, we need to look at what came before.**

**Part 1: What is Your Attachment Style?**

Recall that Clara had the following core belief: "The world is not safe, and I am not safe. People can't be trusted."

Clara can do a great deal to challenge this core belief, to reframe it, to look for evidence, and to gradually rework it into something that helps her life instead of sabotages it. One way to get rid of this belief is to understand how it got there in the first place. We inquire into the past not so we can blame our parents, shrug our shoulders, and say that nothing can be done, but rather so that we can *understand* ... and do better. Just like the gestalt therapists emphasized, we grapple with the past as a way to live more freely and authentically in the present.

When Clara was a year old, her parents divorced. Her mother was so sick with stress and worry, that she was unable to respond to Clara's emotional needs and often got irritated with the child. Though both her parents loved her, the home environment was chaotic and unstable. Clara remembers that in her teen years, she would often anxiously try to think of ways to cheer her mother up, to be good, to win affection.

John Bowlby was a psychotherapist who was the first to propose a theory of childhood attachment, and he would have classified Clara as having an "anxious" attachment style. Bowlby would say that as an adult, Clara's tendency to catastrophize, to worry, and to feel terrified of being abandoned comes from her early childhood experiences of insecurely attaching to her primary caregiver—in this case, her mother.

**According to Bowlby, "attachment" is a lasting, innate psychological connection between children and their caregivers.** In his research, he notices that, when scared, children ordinarily seek consolation from their primary caregiver. Mary Ainsworth later expanded his work with her "strange situation" investigation, which observed twelve- to eighteen-month-olds while they were momentarily left alone and then reunited with their mothers. The research revealed that even at that young age, the infants had characteristic styles of attachment:

- Secure attachment (this is the healthy "normal" mode)

- Dismissive avoidant
- Fearful avoidant
- Disorganized/insecure attachment (later added by Main and Solomon in 1986)

**The theory goes that a person's early attachment style influences all their subsequent relationships, whether that's with friends, family, romantic partners, or colleagues.** It also influences self-concept; identity; behavior; and (as we saw with Clara) a host of core beliefs, expectations, and biases about the world.

Clara's early attachment relationship became a model that was repeated in all her later connections with others. As an adult, Clara finds herself with marriage difficulties, and her attachment style is a big part of that. A theme we'll return to throughout this book is that in self-therapy, there is no way to fix one part of your life without implicating another. Clara began her self-therapy journey by trying to manage her anxiety, but may end that journey taking a more honest look at her relationship patterns and her choices in that area of life.

According to Bowlby and subsequent researchers, all this was set in place in very early life—but with awareness we can change. Let's take a look at these styles.

**Dismissive-Avoidant**

Someone who has adopted a dismissive-avoidant style has a core emotion of painful uncertainty in their relationships, which they deal with by denying their own need. In Bowlby's experiments, these were the children who did not appear distressed when their mothers left them in a strange environment, as though to say, "I don't need her, anyway."

A person with this style may have core beliefs that confirm the basic unreliability of other people, and cognitive biases that work hard to create a feeling of invulnerability and autonomous self-reliance.

**This style is characterized by:**

- Seeming aloof, distant, and withdrawn
- Unlikely to connect at an intimate level, avoiding vulnerability
- Pursuing independence and feeling smothered otherwise

- Finding close involvement with their partners difficult, and feeling anxious about commitment
- Feeling overwhelmed when heavily relied upon
- To escape these feelings, they may retreat either physically or emotionally

**Fearful-Avoidant**

While someone with a dismissive-avoidant attachment style tends to avoid intimacy since it has been so lacking and unreliable in the past, someone with a fearful-avoidant style may have grown up in an environment where the primary caregiver was actively harmful in some way. Whether parents were outright abusive or simply battling their own addictions or emotional pain, it can be incredibly difficult if the person who is meant to care for and love you is also the source of your fear or unhappiness. Understandably, this can create a kind of push/pull ambivalence.

**This style is characterized by:**

- Deep feelings of unworthiness (Being hurt by a loved and needed caregiver

is an unthinkable pain. To "make sense" of it, someone may decide that they were somehow bad or flawed, and that's why they were treated poorly. This doesn't feel good, but it's a way to understand an unbearable situation.)
- Ambivalence in relationships—blowing hot and cold, shifting between being distant and being vulnerable
- Overanalyze microexpressions and body language, monitoring people's emotions very closely to catch any signs of impending danger
- Suspicion and lack of trust
- Being unpredictable

**Disorganized-Insecure Attachment**

This attachment style can result from early caregiving that was highly inconsistent. It's as though the child could never really relax—even when needs were being met, it paid to be vigilant because all that could stop unexpectedly at any moment. For example, someone might have grown up with loving parents, but those parents were both very busy and seldom around. There was love and affection, but it was often given and then retracted. That child grew up with an internalized sense of "what can I do to earn that love back? When is the next bad thing coming and how can I prepare for it?"

**This attachment style is characterized by:**

- Self-sacrificing, people-pleasing behavior
- Hypersensitive to and enormously fearful of rejection—it's like the world is ending!
- Panic about the potential of being abandoned
- They may overcompensate in adult relationships, over-giving and taking on too much responsibility. They may have an unconscious core belief: "In order to be loved, I have to sacrifice my own needs."
- Sacrifice their own needs to maintain relationships
- An inability to feel safe and settled, or to appreciate accomplishments.

You might now be wondering what the normal attachment style looks like. What about when a primary caregiver is available, loving, and responsive to the child's needs?

## Secure attachment

When a growing child feels cared for and loved, they can internalize that feeling of care and self-worth within themselves. If they reliably express their needs and have them met most of the time, they come to trust the people around them and grow up to be broadly stable, balanced adults who by and large have a positive attitude toward the world in general.

## This attachment style is characterized by:

- Feeling secure in relationships
- Are supportive, open, and available in their relationships
- Have healthy self-esteem and intact boundaries
- Are respectful of others
- Find a balance between clingy and aloof, valuing both themselves and others in mature adult relationships
- Have the potential to shift individuals in other attachment styles to a more secure one

Maybe you've noticed that Clara has a mix of fearful-avoidant and insecure attachment styles. While Clara's parents loved her and she loved them, she grew up with a very real sense of their unreliability. Consequently, as a very young child, she internalized the idea that it was her job to figure out how to get her parents to meet her needs. Unconsciously, she worked hard to make others happy, to not have too many needs of her own, to not express her fear or distress—all in the hope that this sacrifice would make her an easier child to love and care for, and prevent people from abandoning her.

Consider again how upset Clara was when her husband was late coming home from work. Understanding her own attachment style gives her a lot of insight into why she felt this way!

**So . . . Can You Change?**

If you've recognized some of yourself in the above descriptions, don't despair. The idea is not to shrug and conclude that nothing can be done. Though our early childhood experiences have an enormous impact on our adult relationships, these patterns are just that—patterns. They're not written in stone. Here are a few ways to start healing attachment wounds and moving toward a healthier attachment style as an adult.

**Take ownership and responsibility for your attachment style.**

As children, we did the best we could with what we had. But as adults, we have the opportunity to become more aware of how we behave. **The more and more aware we become, the more we are responsible for our choices here in the present**. We need to acknowledge the past, understand how it has shaped us, and forgive with compassion. But we also need to take ownership of ourselves and take charge of how we want to live.

If you find that you're an anxiously attached person, your task is to learn to shift inward. For example, instead of focusing on how late her husband is, what could have happened to him, why he didn't call, etc., Clara can turn inward and take responsibility for how *she* is feeling. This is a question of focus. It can be helpful to remind yourself that you simply cannot control others—but with effort, you can moderate and regulate your own internal experience.

If you find that you show a more avoidant attachment style, then you may notice yourself shirking obligations and duties and shying away from bids for intimacy from those around you. It may seem very difficult to meet the needs of other people. Your challenge, then, is to find comfortable ways to meet *both* your needs and theirs. Avoidant people tend to see the motional demands of others as a threat and may feel that they are being asked to give away a part of themselves or undermine themselves to keep people happy. But this is a faulty core belief. The next time you find yourself thinking in black and white, either/or terms ("either they get their way or I do"), try to think in terms of *and*—in what way can you meet their needs and connect with them without compromising your own boundaries? You may need to get better at asking for what you need, meeting your needs yourself, or being more proactive about the kinds of emotional connections you most enjoy.

Relationship problems often occur because we are unconsciously playing out old patterns from the past. We may project onto others our own ingrained habits, or worse, we may deliberately seek out relationships and friendships with only those people who best fit pre-existing molds that were created in childhood. No matter your attachment style, however, you can move on by acknowledging what it is and owning it instead of playing it out over and over with other people.

Clara has an anxious attachment style. Guess what? Her husband has an avoidant one. They are not together by accident—their respective styles complement one another in the worst way possible. Clara is anxious, does too much, overcompensates, and pursues her husband. He in turn shies away from intimacy and commitment and finds Clara's constant neediness alarming. *Together*, they play out their mutual childhood attachment patterns. The cycle can only be broken when they both realize what's happening and take responsibility for it. That means that Clara stops behaving as though her husband's behavior is the cause of her anxiety, and he stops behaving as though her request for reassurance is the cause of him feeling smothered. Then, they can help one another break these old patterns, instead of reinforcing them.

**Bolster your self-esteem.**

Given inadequate or inconsistent parenting, many of us unconsciously come to the sad conclusion that we are somehow inferior and undeserving of complete love. This results in all sorts of self-neglect, self-sabotage, self-criticism, and self-destruction. We may deeply feel that we don't deserve happiness—or if we do, we have to earn it by completely relinquishing our needs and even our rights.

Those who are securely attached, however, have a deep and abiding sense in their worth and general goodness as human beings. They don't think they're perfect, but they are able to forgive their own flaws, to strive to be better without shame and blame, and to show that same compassion to others. Building up your self-esteem is not a shallow endeavor. It cannot be done simply by getting a new haircut, getting a raise, or convincing someone else to compliment you.

Instead, it comes from a deep core of respect and self-regard for yourself as a human being. This is a fundamental, irreducible form of worth you attribute to yourself simply because you are alive—not because you've earned it by doing this or that, or because someone else agreed that you matter, but because you are a human being. Because you are who you are. With this sense of deep worth intact, you are able to forgive yourself, to be patient with yourself as you grow ... not to mention you're able to keep your ego in check and not swing the other direction into narcissism!

- Pay attention to your hygiene, your diet and physical wellbeing, and your daily habits. Take pride in your belongings and your environment.
- Address needs you may be neglecting in yourself—do you need to go to the dentist? Quit smoking? Buy yourself better socks?
- Is there anything it's time you forgave yourself for? What about letting go of anger and blame for other people so you don't have to carry it anymore?
- Reconsider your boundaries. Good self-esteem means protecting your time, your energy, your space, and your resources.
- Remind yourself of your values and commit to centering them more in your life.

- Prioritize your own joy and wellbeing. What really makes you happy? Why not give yourself full permission to pursue that?

## Part 2: Reparenting Yourself

Though the concept may seem a little out there to some, **the principle of reparenting yourself is very simple: It is the act of consciously choosing to provide yourself as an adult with everything you weren't provided for as a child**. What Bowlby and the other attachment theorists discovered is that secure attachment to a caregiver is a human need. But without that need, a child is forced to make compromises and do the best they can with what they have. The result may "work" even if it's not a sustainable and healthy solution long term.

Reparenting heals. If you can give your inner child the love, acceptance, and confidence they needed back then, the idea is that you repair unhealthy attachment styles and build healthier adult relationships. You could waste a lot of time battling poor coping mechanisms and faulty relationship patterns. Or, if you follow the logic of reparenting, you can go back and meet those unmet needs that created the poor coping mechanisms in the first place.

**Your inner child is the part of you that still processes the world like a child**. Your upbringing shapes your unconscious thoughts and feelings, and that in turn shapes the decisions and choices you make. Every childhood event you digest was ingrained in your brain in the past in the form of core beliefs, which affects your life in the present.

Let's take a look now at Nick, who you'll recall battled low motivation, procrastination, and depression. Nick was a very sensitive child. The youngest child in a big and busy family, he walked and talked early and was very bright and vivacious, but his parents were often too exhausted to listen to him prattle endlessly for hours and would sometimes lose their temper with him. Nick has memories of being very creative. He would sing songs, dance around, make up stories, invent things, or spend an entire afternoon making a portrait of the family dog from lawn clippings and glitter stuck to the back of a cereal box.

His parents were well-meaning, but they worked near constantly to provide for Nick and his brothers and sisters, and they seldom had patience for Nick's "naughtiness." More than once, he was scolded for playing around when there were chores to do. Looking back, Nick feels like the thing he internalized from his childhood was the constant message: "Life is hard and difficult! Stop having so much fun!" He also remembered that nothing he created seemed to interest his parents or bring them any joy. By the time he was twelve years old, Nick had stopped all of that. What was the point? In fact, this is something that the grown-up Nick finds himself saying almost daily—"what's the point?"

Of course, we can't say that Nick has depression now just because his parents once forgot to tell him his artwork was pretty. And it's important here to remember that it's not what "really happened" that matters, but what the young Nick *perceived* to be the case. But by doing a little psychological auditing on himself in the present, Nick can start to unpack where his feelings of apathy and low self-worth might have come from.

When it comes to reparenting, there are two theoretical people who are engaged in a kind of dialogue:

> 1. The **adult** person you are right now
> 2. Your **inner child**, who is not who you were back then, but rather a kind of internalized memory of that time in your life, which lives on within you into the present

Of course, these two people are the same person. But by allowing your adult self as it is today to talk to your inner child self, you're able to have some interesting and insightful conversations. Inner child work and reparenting can help you better regulate your emotions and adapt to stress; it can help you develop healthy boundaries, proper routines, and discipline around your own mental wellbeing; it can help you develop genuine self-care, compassion, and forgiveness (not just for yourself but for others, too); and it can reconnect you to the sometimes surprising depths of your own innate joy, wonder, hope, innocence, power, and resilience that you first experienced as a child.

So how do you do it?

Of all the techniques covered in this book, reparenting is arguably the one least suited to practice on our own. A skilled and qualified therapist can help you through all aspects of reparenting yourself, and they can stand in for a parental figure during sessions in a way that may be hard to replicate on your own. That said, there are some exercises and practices that can be done without a therapist, and we'll look at one such exercise below, thinking about how Nick could try it out for himself.

**Step 1: Become aware**

This is not theoretical or purely abstract or verbal work. You are attempting to connect with your inner child—this is not a rational or linear process, and it may not look like anybody else's process. When we were children, our brains were not yet developed and our sense of self was still new and ill-defined. We may have had very limited or distorted awareness that we have long since adjusted for as we've grown up.

The first step is to find some alone time where you won't be disturbed. Sit or lie down somewhere comfortable and take a moment to come into the present and calm your breathing. You can do this exercise when you're upset and emotionally activated, or you can do it when you're calmer—both approaches will yield value. Take a moment to note how your body is feeling, your emotions, and your thoughts. Nick notices that he's a little irritable and tense, with some tightness around his shoulders.

**Step 2: Conjure up your inner child**

There are a few ways to do this. You can close your eyes and, in your imagination, try to recall in as much detail as possible a memory from your childhood, as well as where you fit into this memory. You can use an old photograph or keepsake to help jog your memory. Try to vividly imagine yourself as a child at a certain age—what did you look like, what did you wear, how did you speak? Try to recall the things you were most concerned about. Try to hear your own voice—what kind of things did you say?

Spend your time with this. What you are trying to do is really invoke a crystal-clear image of the younger version of yourself. When you're ready, imagine that this little person is sitting across from you on a chair, or that you have joined them in one of their games. You are approaching this inner child as the current adult version of yourself. For Nick, he imagines himself at twelve years old, sitting in his childhood bedroom. He can remember all the details—the posters on the wall, the way his closet smelled, the color of his school bag in the corner . . .

**Step 3: Listen**

Now it's time to introduce yourself to your inner child and open a dialogue. Imagine that this inner child you're meeting is someone you've never met before. At the same time, imagine that you are the kindest, wisest, and most caring adult possible, here in the present. What should you talk about? Well, that's up to your inner child to decide! The best way to find out is to ask:

*"How do you feel right now?"*
*"What's bothering you?"*
*"What makes you happy?"*
*"What do you need?"*

*"Are you getting the things you need?"*
*"What do you wish would happen right now?"*
*"What do you really want to say?"*

Ask your inner child these questions and be genuinely curious about the answers. Maybe our inner child is hostile and suspicious. *Who are you and why are you asking so many questions?* In that case, be kind and wise—tell your inner child that you're here, you're listening, and you genuinely want to know more about them.

Admittedly, Nick thinks the whole exercise is a little cheesy, but when he gets to this stage of the process, he is very surprised to find that his inner child bursts into tears almost immediately. "What's wrong?" Nick asks, and the child explains that he feels so completely stupid and nothing he does is right and he hates himself. Nick is very taken aback. He asks more questions, listening completely to the answers without arguing, interrupting, or interpreting. Nick is also surprised to find how upset he is to meet this child. He feels sad for him, and protective. Who could look at a child and call them stupid? How could it be that this innocent child in front of him hates himself?

**Step 4: Reparent**

The goal is to figure out what this child needs and to give it to them. Nick sees it all at once: Young Nick is a small, sensitive boy who simply needs to be told that he is worthwhile, that he has value, and that the things he creates and does are welcome in the world. He needs a big fat hug and the reassurance that he will always be cherished and cared for. He needs to be comforted and told that there *is* a point, that people are listening to him, and that he belongs here in the world as much as anyone else. Nick bends down to hug the child, and they play together for a while. The child shows him some interesting new things he's been working on, and Nick listens with interest. Then, he says goodbye, promising to come back and visit later.

What does your inner child most need? And how can you give it to them?

Maybe they're afraid and need reassurance that someone is there to protect them.
Maybe they want to be spontaneous and innocent and silly.
Maybe they need a little discipline and for someone to tell them no!

Maybe they need you to keep your promise to them.

Maybe they're just lonely and need you to listen.

Maybe they want to play but everyone is too busy and distracted.

Maybe they need someone to apologize to them and make things right.

Maybe they need to say what they know is true and be believed.

For Nick, his inner child had become sad and disillusioned. He needed someone to care about him and what he was doing and show interest in him. So, that's what Nick did.

## Step 5: Applying what you learn

When Nick comes out of this self-parenting session, it's not the end of the process. Simply encountering and listening to your inner child will trigger enormous shifts in you, but it's also worth deliberately taking what you learn and applying it to your everyday life. In Nick's case, he discovered, for the first time in his life, what it felt like *not* to be apathetic, self-critical, and pessimistic. Whenever he felt himself slipping into negative self-talk and inner criticism, he would remind himself of that desperately unhappy 12-year-old crying in his childhood bedroom. Would he say such harsh and unkind things to that 12-year-old? If not, then why was he telling himself that?

Nick remembered all the things his younger self needed to hear and wrote them down, transforming them into affirmations:

*You are worthwhile.*
*You have value.*
*You belong.*
*You have skills and gifts and talents, and these are welcome in the world.*
*It is never a waste of time to pursue your dreams.*
*You are worth listening to.*
*You deserve to be treated with respect and care.*

Nick places these affirmations somewhere he can see them every day and recites them often. Something starts to shift inside him. The next time he feels depressed and is thinking about ordering in some junk food and wasting the afternoon on a gaming binge, he feels just how at odds this behavior is with the affirmations he said just a few hours earlier. Is junk food and gaming really what he needs? Is he taking care of himself and respecting his gifts and worth by doing that?

Nick finds that he has even become a little protective over that inner child. When he meets up with an old family friend who playfully teases him about his lack of a proper job and insinuates that Nick will always be a loser, Nick instantly draws a boundary and calls his friend out. In time, Nick finds that he is less and less tolerant of things that lower his feelings of self-worth, and people who do not listen to him. His big lightbulb moment comes when he realizes that the worst offender for this is *himself*—does he want to continue lowering his own worth and refusing to listen to himself?

You don't have to go all out to benefit from the principle of inner child work and reparenting. You can simply treat yourself with the same care and respect as you would a vulnerable child who depends on you.

- Keep your promises, keep your word
- Say no to things that are unhealthy and make you unhappy
- Don't let people bully or undermine you

- Have enough discipline to stick to wholesome routines and habits
- Find time for joy and relaxation
- Trust yourself and value your own opinion

**Part 3: Transactional Analysis**

When we reparent, we are deliberately making use of the dynamic between parent and child in order to heal past wounds. But there is another common psychological theory that draws on these parent/child dynamics—specifically the ones that already exist.

Let's go back to Thea, who was trying to navigate the transition to retired life. Her core belief was that she had no value unless she worked hard and provided value to others—so when she stopped working, she suddenly felt aimless, guilty, and ashamed. Thea's inner voice was like a nagging, critical parent: "Are you sure that's a good idea? You're being lazy again. Why haven't you figured this out yet?"

This, in fact, was also the way Thea treated others. She was always the serious and responsible one, always there to pick up other people's mess, to do the boring administration work, to be the designated driver, and to basically play the role of parent. It's probably no surprise that Thea attracted a lot of people into her life that wanted to, well, play the child role!

In the 1960s, Canadian psychiatrist Dr. Eric Berne created the theory of transactional analysis (TA). **This psychological theory explores the modes people take on when they interact with others, and the kinds of "games" and scripts they play in social settings. Games are patterns of social behavior that play out in predictable ways.** These unconscious patterns were developed in childhood but are also heavily influenced by culture, history, context, etc.

According to TA, ego states are clusters of feelings that influence people's communication style. There are three ego states (shortened to PAC): parent, adult, and child.

The **parent** is the mode based on introjected (i.e., taken within the self) parental figures and forms from a person's early life. A parent can fall into one of two paradigms; they can be controlling and powerful, making demands and setting limits and rules, or they can be nurturing, protective, wise, and supportive. The way that you enter parent mode is determined by your own experiences of your parents growing up.

You can tell that someone is in the parent ego state when they appear to be talking *down* to others, using terms like "you should," and adopting a tone of voice and mannerisms that suggest a kind of authority. This is definitely the ego state that Thea most often finds herself in! Whether she's authoritarian or kind and nurturing, she usually takes on a mothering role for others.

The **adult** is the system of here-and-now analysis. The adult can be understood as a bit like a computer trying to logically solve problems. This mode is assertive, practical, neutral, and rational, and everything it does is embedded in reality. When people are healthy, balanced, and unburdened psychologically, they naturally enter the adult ego state. People in the adult state are open and curious and base their decisions on data from the here and now rather than distortions from the past.

The **child** relates to experiences of the self from the past, and it's not dissimilar from the inner child we've discussed so far. There are different forms of child mode. The "adapted child" responds to parent demands either compliantly or rebelliously rather than to its own needs. They try hard to please others and desperately want to be liked, so they comply readily with others' wishes and can come across as submissive, timid, or lacking boundaries. On the other hand, they may make a show of flouting rules and boundaries, pushing strongly against them. In either case, the behavior is always primarily in response to the parent's demands.

The free or "natural child" responds primarily to its own needs and is spontaneous. They're intelligent, creative, and joyful but may be inconsiderate of other people's needs. The "somatic child" reflects a time in childhood when body issues were prominent. A person fully identified with the somatic child ego state may have a host of physical complaints rather than psychological ones. Incidentally, Nick may often find himself in this mode, especially when he's sulking on the sofa, saying he doesn't want to do any chores!

What's the point of knowing all this?

Traditionally, TA was used as a way for people to understand human interaction and communication. It provided a useful framework to better recognize misunderstandings and conflict so they can be minimized. But in the self-therapy context, the theory is useful for helping each person understand the ego state with which they approach other people, and how this impacts the way they interact and communicate.

A person doesn't live in the same ego state forever. They can switch states depending on the context, the task, etc. But with awareness, you can recognize when you are slipping into rebellious child mode or becoming too much of a bossy parent type (like Thea might), and consciously decide if your needs would be better met by going into adult instead. Just like cognitive distortions and incorrect core beliefs, ego states are there because on some level, we believe they will help us meet our needs. Usually, though, they don't!

We all adopt different ego states in every conversation or interaction we have. In an overall relationship that spans several events and conversations, and on a broader level, there may be lifelong patterns of routinely defaulting to a favored state. You can gain deeper insight into yourself by

1. Noticing what role you are playing in every conversation as it unfolds
2. Noticing the recurring patterns in your relationships
3. Noticing your overarching tendencies throughout life
4. Finally, noticing your own attitude toward yourself

Thea takes these ideas into her own life and starts to notice that she is quite often in parent mode. Sometimes she's a nurturing parent; sometimes she's a critical, judgmental one who likes to control and domineer. She starts to see all the relationships in her life, past and present, in a new light. All the people she's had difficult and conflictual connections with have tended to be people who often went into rebellious child mode. Did Thea attract these people into her life, or did her tendency to play the role of parent force others to play the role of naughty children? Truthfully, it's probably both!

Most importantly, Thea realizes that she plays out this same dynamic with herself *intrapsychically*. It is as though the stern and critical inner parent is always stepping in to make a snide comment about the rebellious and strong-willed child. Piggybacking on her core beliefs that tell her she doesn't have any worth unless she's working hard, she adopts an attitude where she freely criticizes herself and others for being lazy, unmotivated, and lacking discipline and direction (you can imagine how much conflict she'd have with poor Nick!).

But it's only when she can come out of that mode and go in the adult ego state that things will start to genuinely change. The way to do this is to become aware and then to gently challenge yourself to find the adult perspective instead. For example, Thea is chatting one day with an old school friend. This friend has not retired yet, and in fact doesn't plan to. Thea finds herself saying things like:

"Oh, that sounds great! You should just remember to top up a little pension pot anyway, just in case."

"Take it from someone who *has* retired: it's not what you think. Let me tell you how it is . . ."

"Well done for you. I've always admired how disciplined and dedicated you are."

"Are you sure you've thought clearly about how the next ten or twenty years will play out, though?"

"You're so smart, though. Are you sure this job will be challenging enough for you?"

Now, all of the above may fit seamlessly into pleasant conversation and is not a problem as such. But go back and read them again and see if you can hear the parent ego state—both the supportive version and the critical version! Because of Thea's own core beliefs, assumptions, and personal psychological filters, she is adopting the role of perpetual parent. She has taken it upon herself to be the expert ("let me tell you how it really is . . .") and is offering both praise and criticism from a position of assumed authority and parental concern.

If Nick from our earlier example paid attention to the way he spoke in interactions, he'd probably notice patterns for his own ego state. Can you guess which one?

"God, just five more minutes, and then I'll get up."
"I know I shouldn't have pizza for dinner *again*, but to hell with it."
"The doctor said my blood work came back just fine. That was super helpful, right? Idiot."
"That's just your opinion."
"Look, I'll try, but I'm not making any promises..."

Again, any one of these phrases alone doesn't mean much, but as a whole, they might hint at a recurring pattern of rebellious child ego state. Consider the last one: "I'll try, but no promises." There is the acknowledgment of external life demands, but already there is the preparation to avoid, shirk, or rebel against them.

Now, can you imagine what would happen if Thea and Nick had a conversation together? In fact, try to imagine that Thea is Nick's mom—it's easy to, right? Eric Berne, the founder of TA, would say that when these two get together, they have compatible and mutually reinforcing styles that trap the both of them in a mutual pattern—what he called a "game."

One of Berne's most recognizable games is one he calls "yes, but." Take a read and see if you have encountered this game before. Perhaps you've even played both parts of the script!

Nick: "I just wish I knew why I always felt so fatigued all the time."

Thea: "I keep telling you, it's your diet. You need to test for vitamin deficiencies, with the way you eat."

Nick: "Yeah, but I told you already I'm not on that health insurance anymore."

Thea: "Well, that doesn't matter. You can just get a test done yourself. They don't cost much."

Nick: "You can get the cheaper ones, but they're not reliable. I read an article about it. You need to pay up if you want an accurate one."

Thea: "Okay, fine. I'll pay. How much are they?"

Nick: "No, you are *not* paying for anything. It's not a vitamin deficiency, anyway."

Thea: "Maybe if you just took a multivitamin anyway, a good one, just to be sure you're covering all your bases..."

Nick: "I already take one and it does nothing."

Thea: "Okay, sure, but maybe try a different one, then?"

Nick: "Yes, but..."

Are you getting a good idea of the rules of this game? Thea, the parent, plays the role of trying to solve the problem of Nick, who plays the role of the rebellious child, who has a problem that cannot (will not) ever be solved. According to Berne, games like this can carry on indefinitely and will only change when one of the parties changes their ego state.

Let's imagine that Thea is learning more about herself and more about the automatic parent role she takes all the time. Let's say Nick is indeed her son and that she is at her wit's end trying to help him. Knowing more about her own attachment style, her core beliefs, and the roles she takes in interactions, Thea realizes the part she is playing in continuing the drama with her son, Nick. How does anything change? Not by them playing another round of "yes, but." Instead, it changes when both of them can come into the adult ego state.

Now, there are many, many different games that Berne outlined (it's worth reading his 1964 book, *Games People Play* to get an overview), but what matters is simply that you start to pay attention to the recurring and unconscious patterns that may be going on in your own life. **What role do you play to keep these stereotyped interactions going?**

Are you always playing at being helpless, challenging others to come and save you—only so you can come up with reasons why they can't?

Are you the eternal fixer-upper who is always finding someone who plays at being impossible to fix?

Do you play the game Berne called "Please Don't Kick Me"?

> *This is played by men whose social manner is equivalent to wearing a sign that reads "Please Don't Kick Me." The temptation is almost irresistible, and when the natural result follows, he cries piteously, "But the sign says, 'don't kick me.'" Then he adds incredulously, "Why does this always happen to me?"*

Do you often find yourself playing a game of "Let's you and him fight," where you encourage two suitors to compete for you?

Are you often playing the role of a persecuting and nitpicking lawyer who hides his attacks in passive aggression? Or are you most often the helpless victim who secretly doesn't mind being picked on because it absolves him from having to make his own choices?

TA is a fascinating lens through which to look at human interactions and, if you're honest with yourself, can provide rich insight into your most automatic and knee-jerk behaviors.

In the next conversation you're in, ask yourself:

*What role am I playing? And the other person?*
*Are we playing out a script we've gone through before? What's the payoff for both of us?*
*Am I in parent, adult, or child ego state? And them?*
*Is this game helping me achieve what I want? If not, how would I like to change things?*

**Summary**:

- If we want to know who we are now and why we are that way, we need to look at what came before, i.e., our childhoods. Bowlby outlined different styles of infant attachment (secure attachment, dismissive-avoidant, and fearful-avoidant) and showed how each shaped the adult's relationship patterns. We can become aware of and take responsibility for our attachment styles as adults, in the present. Working on self-esteem and having relationships with people with secure attachment styles are ways we can mitigate our early programming.

- You can also heal wounds from the past by "reparenting," which is consciously choosing to provide yourself as an adult with everything you weren't provided with as a child. With visualization, our present-day adult goes back to engage with and heal their inner child. Become aware, conjure up the inner child, and dialogue with them, truly listening to what they say. Then commit to giving them what they need.
- It's important to apply the lessons learned in real life—for example, by setting boundaries or embracing healthier habits and routines.
- Eric Berne's transactional analysis is another way to understand our ingrained and stereotypical relationship patterns. Berne outlined three ego states we can occupy: parent, child, and adult. These unconscious patterns shape the "games" we play, but with conscious awareness, we can shift into a more neutral adult ego state.
- It's worthwhile asking yourself what role you most often play and what games recur in your life so that you can consciously choose something different.

## Chapter 4: Anxiety, Trauma, and Coping

### Part 1: Cognitive Defusion Exercises

We have spent time exploring who we are, what we're made of, and how we got to be made that way. But even once we have gained great self-awareness and are conscious of how we work at the every level, does that mean we never experience any discomfort, stress, or adversity in life? Of course not!

In this final chapter, we're looking at ways to use self-therapy not simply to deepen our self-knowledge, but also to tackle more singular problems that emerge in everyday life. **No matter how well adjusted we are, we will all encounter stress, disappointment, loss, or even trauma.**

**Genuine resilience comes from knowing how to manage and cope.**

In CBT (cognitive behavioral therapy), the focus is on becoming aware of and changing negative or unhelpful beliefs, as we saw in the first chapter. But sometimes, this can be extremely difficult to do. If you're stuck in the middle of a crisis or dealing with something who is extremely challenging, you're not likely to have the presence of mind to sit down with a journal and rationally pick through your thoughts!

But what we can do at crisis points like this is use a technique from ACT, or acceptance and commitment therapy. It's a process called "cognitive defusion," and it's essentially a way to *let go of internal resistance or struggle.* With CBT, we might actively engage a faulty or distorted belief and work with it; with cognitive defusion, we don't engage with it at all—we simply find ways to accept, release, and let go of the struggle that tells us: "This is a problem! I hate this! It has to stop."

Cognitive defusion, which was first called cognitive distancing by Dr. Aaron Beck, the founder of cognitive therapy, is a way that

**we can *choose* how to relate to our thoughts and feelings in different situations.** The key insight of cognitive defusion is that we can have emotions and thoughts *without necessarily reacting to them.*

To understand how it all works, let's consider what Beck understood as cognitive *fusion*—i.e., being fused with your emotional and experiential perception. In this state of mind, your thoughts and your direct experiences get so mixed up that you can't tell them apart. A big part of what makes us human is our constant appraisal, interpretation, and reaction to reality around it, filtered through our unique perspectives. We take our experiences and put them into groups, break them down, judge them, compare them to others, and formulate expectations and conclusions. All of these mental processes, however, contribute to fusion—the state of being completely *identified and bonded with* our experiences.

This is what the mind does naturally, and it is a good way to solve most problems. In fact, our cognitive abilities can sometimes lead to the desirable and satisfying state of flow, in which there is no difference between the self and an interesting, challenging task. Our collective achievements in science, technology, and the arts are based on this form of thinking.

But often, these labels and judgments are negative and global, like "I'm worthless. I'm a failure," "He's selfish," or "They're mean." Then, these judgments are no longer thoughts we are having or feelings we are temporarily experiencing—they become a *part* of us. They come to define us and our experience. A simple example will illustrate. Remember Jamie, whose bipolar-style mood swings stemmed from a deep sense of his own inadequacy? When Jamie is experiencing a high, he is totally fused with that feeling of elation. He *is* that euphoria. He loses all perspective and dives deep into that feeling.

Similarly, when he is down in the dumps, he is so identified with that feeling that he completely forgets how he felt just a week ago. He doesn't say, "I'm feeling pretty depressed at the moment," but rather, "I'm a depressed person. The world is nothing but despair, and I'm a total failure." See the difference?

**Fused**: we are totally subsumed, identified, and fused with our thoughts and feelings.

**Defused**: the thoughts and feelings are there, but they do not completely define us or our situation forever.

Jamie often rode a hellish rollercoaster of emotions because he was firmly fused with those emotions. It's like being chained to that rollercoaster car, dragged along with every rise and fall. But being defused is more like watching the rollercoaster car from somewhere far removed, safely on the ground. You can see that your emotions are rising and falling, but that doesn't mean you have to completely surrender and go along with them.

This is where the ACT notion of acceptance comes in. **When we push against and resist a particular thought or feeling, we *are fused with it as when we grasp hold of it*.** For example, if Jamie notices a dark mood beginning to creep over him, and he unconsciously says, "No, no, no, a depression is coming. This is bad thing!" he is just as embroiled with that sensation, just as powerless, as when he decides to prolong any "good" feelings that come his way.

This is important—Defusion is not the same as resistance. Rather, *resistance and clinging are both forms of fusion*, two sides of the same coin.

So what does defusion look like? Does it mean we have to be bland, empty, emotionless? Not at all. We have all the same reactions, knee-jerk responses, and spontaneous feelings and thoughts as we always do. But when we are defused, we understand thoughts as thoughts. We see feelings as feelings. We understand that even though we are scared or angry or sad, it doesn't mean that we will always feel that way. We also understand that just because we experience something, it doesn't mean we are compelled to act. This is truly liberating—feelings and thoughts are just that. Feelings and thoughts. That's all. Just temporary electrochemical activity in the brain. Just a momentary ripple in the pond.

They are nothing unless we choose to fuse with them and allow ourselves to be compelled by them. ACT reminds us that we have that choice.

Using the ACT model, we can deliberately practice defusing from our emotions and thoughts. Importantly, we are not getting rid of them (remember, resistance is just another form of fusion), but rather changing our relationship to them. Here are four key techniques to try the next time you are feeling overwhelmed by negative emotions.

**Technique #1: Distancing**

Think of fusion and defusion in terms of distance: too "close" and we are fused, but with a little distance, we can gain perspective and some breathing room. We are not the same thing as our thoughts and feelings. There is a little gap between them and us. If we take on an *observer* role, we are no longer in the active *player* role, and we automatically create some psychological distance.

How do we create that distance? There are many ways, but try the following:

1. Just pause and become aware
2. Zoom in on a negative or overwhelming thought or emotion
3. Try to get a sense of how "close" you currently are. Do you fully believe the

story that you are telling yourself? Are you immersed in it?

4. Add some distance. You could use language, for example, by saying, "My brain is having the thought that . . ." or, "There is a feeling happening right now . . ." Additionally, instead of saying, "I'm a failure," you gain distance by saying, "My brain is having the thought that I'm a failure right now."

5. Adding "today" or "right now" adds some temporal distance—i.e., you phrase things so that the current phenomenon is understood to be temporary. Instead of, "I'm struggling," you can say, "I'm struggling at the moment." This adds some distance because it implies there will be a time when this emotion or thought will stop.

6. Use visualization and imagine the thought or feeling as a picture, symbol, or even a little cartoon character. Maybe you see your anxiety as a literal brick wall that spells out the letters ANXIETY. Or maybe you picture your critical inner voice as a nagging little insect that's following you around, speaking in a squeaky voice.

So, for Jamie, when he notices that he's sinking into a depression again, he doesn't resist, nor does he sink down immediately with that feeling. Instead, he tries to stand outside that feeling, adopting the perspective of someone who is watching the event unfold. "Oh, I can feel that my mood is dropping a little today." Even saying "my mood" is dropping rather than "I" am feeling depressed creates a sense of distance. The depressed mood may still come, and it may be as strong as ever, only now Jamie is outside that storm rather than right at its center.

**Technique #2: Labeling**

When we are fused with a thought, it seeps into everything and feels exactly identical to reality. We may not know what we are experiencing, only that we are experiencing. However, when we put a label on something, we can immediately see that it is something that has a reality outside of us and that it is just a "thing." Have you ever noticed how thoughts and feelings seem so big and intimidating, and yet, once you share them verbally with someone else, they seem so much smaller somehow? This is the power of labeling at work.

How to label:

1. Simply describe what is happening. Slow down, become aware, and try to just describe what you're perceiving—without judgment or evaluation. Consult your five senses and see what data they are sending you. Jamie may pause one afternoon and think, "I notice a light, fluttery feeling in my stomach. My jaw feels tight. I seem to be moving around very quickly. I can hear the sound of my own voice, and it's higher pitched than normal."
2. Once you've done this, you may also find yourself describing actions and events, i.e., how you are engaging with the stimuli around you. "My mind is noticing a fluttery feeling in my stomach. My mind is telling me a story about what that means. I notice I'm having a memory about this feeling from the past. I notice I'm thinking of my father . . ."

If you have been practicing becoming aware in this way for some time, you might recognize old patterns and habits, and you may even be able to say things like, "I can see that I'm catastrophizing again," or, "I am having a cognitive distortion." You might be surprised to find just how repetitive your most stressful and unpleasant thoughts really are, and that if you only pay attention, many times it's exactly the same old thought popping up that you've had before. This can be an interesting realization—that you are not responding spontaneously to the situation in the present, but have merely been triggered by something, and you run off along the same mental track that you habitually do. It can be quite the insight to realize that how you're feeling actually has nothing to do with the situation you thought it did, but is more accurately an old script from the past that's playing out yet again.

**Technique #3: Leaves on a stream meditation**

Gaining psychological distance and giving labels to your experiences are things you do "in the heat of the moment." The following technique can be used in this way, too, but it's also a great daily practice that will flex your defusion muscles and help you master the ability to step outside of your perspective when you're feeling overwhelmed. You can do this any time. It's simple to do.

1. As with any mindfulness or meditative practice, sit somewhere comfortable where you won't be disturbed, close your eyes, and spend a moment becoming aware of your breath.
2. In your mind's eye, picture that you are sitting beside a peaceful flowing stream in a lovely forest. If it's easier, open your eyes and rest your gaze softly on some fixed point while you imagine this.
3. Now, imagine that your mind is also like this stream, and it is flowing along with it. You will notice that as your mind flows, thoughts and feelings and perceptions pop up automatically. With a calm, detached attitude, have a look at each one as it appears. Now, pick up a leaf from the forest floor, imagine placing your thought on this leaf, and then float the leaf on the stream and watch as it carries the thought gently away, out of your sight.
4. Another thought will pop up. It doesn't matter if it's a "good" thought or a "bad" one. It could be a thought, a feeling, or something neutral like, "I wonder if I'm doing the exercise right?" Look at these just the same and put each one on its own leaf and send it down the stream. Even if you think, "There are too many thoughts!

Gah, I can't keep up!" then guess what? That's also a thought. Onto a leaf it goes . . .

5. The stream goes at its own fixed pace. Nothing speeds up or slows down. You are not trying to get rid of a thought, and you're not holding on to it, wishing to keep it for a little longer. They just come and go at the pace of the river's flow.
6. Some thoughts might get "stuck," or they may seem to pop up again and again. That's okay. You might imagine that it swirls around a little on an eddy or gets snagged on the riverbank. Gently nudge it so it flows again. Watch as it goes until you can't see it anymore. Give each thought its proper due and then let it go.
7. You may occasionally get sidetracked and distracted by a thought and forget the exercise you're doing. No matter! The moment you're aware, come back to it. Even if you feel irritated or upset by the detour, place that on a leaf—no matter how big or small a feeling, it will fit comfortably on a leaf, and it *will* pass.

Practice this exercise daily and you will be surprised at how you can change your own relationship to the thoughts that pop into your mind. Jamie does this for a few weeks and finds that he is less reactive, less "up and down." One day, he notices that something that ordinarily would have triggered him just seems to sit there, and he watches it, non-reactive. He thinks, "Oh, there's that trigger again. I guess I could follow it and go all along that same old path as I always do. But I think instead I'll just watch it. It will go before too long." And he's right.

## Part 2: The Art of "Coping Ahead"

Many of the techniques covered in earlier chapters happen *after* you've already experienced a particular thought or emotion. We talk about coping and resilience, but this applies to things that are already done and dusted—coping after the fact. But if we are aware of these patterns, we can step in and stop them before they happen.

Coping "ahead" is a way to break patterns. This is a technique that comes from the therapeutic modality of dialectical behavioral therapy, or DBT. **Using this approach, you walk yourself through a mental rehearsal of a possible future situation.** The idea is that if you are able to anticipate a challenging scenario, you give yourself the opportunity to practice what you will do in that event *before* it occurs.

This way, you develop competence and agency. Beyond that, you are required to have considerable forethought and honesty when thinking about your strategy for dealing with emerging situations, rather than just passively waiting to see how you will react in the moment. When a crisis hits or a challenge rears its head, it may be incredibly difficult to respond there and then in a calm, rational, and level-headed way—even if you ordinarily are a very balanced and competent person! Don't make life harder for yourself. If you notice a recurring pattern, the upside of this is that you are empowered to prepare in advance for how you want to cope with it. This is much, much easier than trying to strong-arm your way through difficult moments through willpower alone.

So how do you cope ahead?

First, you need to **think about the kind of situations that typically prove difficult for you**. Clara, who you already know is learning to deal with her anxiety and fear of abandonment, has identified a list of situations that tend to trigger her feelings of panic and catastrophic thinking:

*When saying goodbye to someone.*
*When people are late or cancel at the last minute.*
*When someone is doing the "silent treatment" or not paying attention.*
*When somebody loses their temper and starts shouting.*
*When two close friends or family members are fighting with one another.*

She also makes a list of people she most tends to feel anxious around (her mother-in-law, doctors, a particular person on social media) and times/periods that are most stressful and difficult (Mondays, the time before her birthday, evenings when she's most tired).

After a long and bitter experience, Clara knows that these situations and people tend to activate her core belief ("the world isn't safe; I'm not safe") and set off a range of unhelpful cognitive distortions. She knows that she then tends to behave in desperate and irrational ways. When things reach this point, she is often so fused with these feelings and thoughts that it's difficult to pull back and gain perspective. But, if she knows this beforehand, she can plan ahead and help herself before the situation spirals out of control.

The next step is to **tune into your inner sage**. If you've tried some of the exercises in this book, you've already been doing this. Your inner sage is the wisest part of you that always has your best interest at heart. This is your higher self, your intuition, your intelligence, and your real, best self, in whatever form makes most sense to you. This is the frame of mind that works to *counterbalance* the automatic, unconscious, often unhealthy emotional mind.

When Clara's husband came home a little late from work, she instantly blew up at him when he did arrive, causing a rift. She felt embarrassed by her extreme behavior and regretted it. For so many people, much damage can be done when the overly emotional mind has free reign and acts before the wiser mind can weigh in. Your inner sage is there to help you proactively plan how you want to behave in certain situations. Then when the situation arises, you may feel those strong emotions, but there is always that little voice of the sage who is standing off to the side, saying, "Remember what we said we were going to do? Let's do that now." Merely being in conscious control of your own experience this way can be enough to break the spell of powerful and overwhelming negative emotions. In that small gap that is opened up, you give yourself the chance to make different choices.

## Four Steps to Letting Your Inner Sage Take Charge

### Step 1: Describe the situation

First, gain clarity over the situation you are trying to prepare for. Label it. Gain as much psychological distance from it as you can and get very familiar with it. However, you are not seeing this situation from a fused point of view, but rather neutrally. Imagine you are describing the scenario to a disinterested third party, or as though you were writing a newspaper report. Just the facts.

Try also to predict how you will be in that scenario. Name the expected emotions, thoughts, and actions. Clara, for example, finds going to the doctor extremely stressful, especially when that doctor withholds information or is generally dismissive or absent. She explores this situation and paints a picture in her mind of how it might play out: She gets panicky when kept in the dark, then imagines all kinds of nightmare scenarios that are really just mountains out of molehills. She keeps her eye on the facts, though: This feeling isn't strictly warranted.

**Step 2: Identify the necessary skills**

Okay, so how could you possibly cope with such a situation if it should happen? Be as specific as possible and be creative. You might realize how comfortable it is to solve problems before they're "real"! Would you need to take a timeout? Distract yourself? Call on someone for help? Find more information and support? Clara realizes that the thing that would most help her in her case is to speak up for herself and be assertive, asking for updates from the doctor and to be told what is happening and why. This cuts down on anxiety rumination.

**Step 3: Rehearse yourself coping**

So far so good. Next, try it out. Use the power of visualization to mentally rehearse not just the situation but how you will cope with it. Be vivid and detailed. See yourself *inside* the situation, not merely watching it from afar. Imagine it literally unfolding now, in the present, rather than hypothetically. And then conjure the details—who you're with, what they're saying, how you feel, what you're doing, etc.

Clara pictures in minute detail the consulting room of her local GP practice. She imagines herself feeling nervous and unsure, but rehearses the moment when she says, "Actually, can I please ask you to explain that more? I'm not sure I understand." She feels the strength of her assertive voice. She rehearses nodding her head, asking further questions. She pictures herself leaving the doctor's office, feeling satisfied that she spoke up.

Clara might do this a few times, and she even throws a few curveballs in. What happens if the doctor is a little rude? What happens if they shrug and tell her they don't know? She rehearses all this too. The great thing about this technique is that you get to feel out the contours of a potentially stressful situation all on your own terms. Clara can speed things up, slow them down, or rewind them so she can try again. She can practice dealing with the things she is most afraid of—and she can ramp up that threat as and when she is ready. As someone with a tendency to catastrophize, Clara's mind often jumps to the worst possible outcome. But she uses her visualization to safely address these ideas on her own terms.

What's the worst that could happen? Well, she mentally rehearses that, too. She pictures the scariest and most upsetting doctor's appointment she can . . . and fleshes out all the ways she would cope with that. By doing so, she prepares ahead, but she also reminds herself that she does actually possess valuable skills, resources, and coping mechanisms. In the heat of the moment, we can all forget our own strengths and forget that we are resilient and capable. Sometimes, we feel better able to cope with whatever comes our way simply because we have reminded ourselves that we *can* manage and have that confidence.

**Step 4: Relax**

As you're doing this rehearsal, remember to practice a relaxed state of mind so that you pair up the difficult situation with a feeling of calm and collected control. Try to maintain a sense of calm while you rehearse, but afterward too. Stretch, take a deep breath, give yourself a pat on the back, and take a little break—rehearsing this way is hard work!

But if you can practice this with your worst fears and your most disorienting triggers, you will give yourself the gift of facing it next time feeling fully prepared. You will instantly see the situation and be *familiar* with it. Sure, it will still be stressful or unpleasant. But you will not be swept away by this. Instead, your body and mind will already know what to do and slip into it automatically. If you need to, verbally remind yourself that you have done this before. "Inner sage, help me out—what do I do here?" Take a deep breath and pause. In that little space that you create, you will find that you can cope.

In a way, coping ahead is not dissimilar from cognitive defusion—the only difference is that you are laying a plan for the future for how you will continue to maintain distance from overwhelming and stressing thoughts, and constantly keep in touch with your own power to choose how you will behave no matter what your feelings and thoughts and no matter how challenging the situation.

## Part 3: Systematic Desensitization

**Systematic desensitization therapy is a type of behavioral therapy used to treat things like anxiety, phobias, OCD, and PTSD.** The idea is that people can be conditioned to avoid or be repelled by a certain stimulus, in just the same way that Pavlov's dogs were conditioned to salivate whenever the bell rang and signaled that food was coming. But if these associations can be conditioned, the theory goes, that means they can also be deconditioned.

So, for example, in the past, you might have had a very embarrassing and uncomfortable encounter where you met someone new. Your brain made the link: Meeting someone new equals painful feelings of embarrassment. The next time you were due to meet someone new, you instantly felt aversion and worry, as though in preparation for the stimulus (meeting someone new) to produce the same response (feelings of embarrassment).

Scientists and psychologists have been studying conditioning for a long time, but you don't have to have an extreme phobia to be subject to its basic principles. If you have places and objects that remind you of a bad time in your past or a specific person you dislike, if you find yourself irrationally avoiding certain situations, or if your bad moods always seem to happen at particular times of day, then you may be experiencing the power of conditioning and association.

**Systematic desensitization is a way to use counterconditioning—i.e., to consciously decide which stimuli to expose ourselves to and how to manage and "train" our responses to them.** Very broadly, the idea is simple: Expose yourself to the thing you fear in small quantities while you link the experience to feelings of relaxation. Then ramp up the stimulus and repeat until you have learned to tolerate the stimulus without going into anxious "fight or flight" mode.

This process is usually done with a trained therapist, but you can do it yourself if you pay close attention to the two ingredients required:

1. Graded exposure, i.e., moving through a hierarchy of stimuli
2. Relaxation

The key is to combine these effectively. If you are merely exposing yourself to things that freak you out, you will only reinforce those pathways and become more effective at freaking out! Similarly, if you only relax, you are not really challenging yourself to learn a different response. You need to *pair* the relaxation with the graded exposure for this technique to have any effect.

Take a classic example: You're afraid of spiders.

1. You construct a graded exposure "ladder" going from one to ten.
2. One is thinking about spiders, two is looking at a picture of a spider, ten is letting a spider walk on your hand, and so on.
3. You start with one and think about spiders.
4. As you think about spiders, you employ your relaxation techniques.

5. When you are able to remain relaxed *while* thinking about spiders, then you move on to level two.
6. You move up the ladder until you can let a spider walk on you happily, with no problem.

As you can see, the theory is pretty simple. Let's take a closer look at how you might use these principles in your own life to break bad habits, overcome fears and phobias, and tackle triggers from traumatic events in your past. We'll return to Nick, who, having hunkered down at home with depression for months, has developed a mild form of agoraphobia—a fear of crowds, open spaces, and leaving the house.

The problem set in gradually. Every time he went out to go shopping or meet friends, he found that he felt depressed and anxious. He hated people seeing how much weight he'd gained, he hated people's nosy questions about how his job hunt was going, and he hated the noisy crowds that only seemed to drive home his feelings of isolation and annoyance with life in general. And so, without him realizing it, he began to associate the world outside his home with negative feelings, and the world inside as safe, comfortable, and happy.

But he needs to break this association. He needs to get outside, exercise, volunteer, connect with friends, and more. But throwing himself into a busy social life all at once will likely only make him feel worse, and then the association will be strengthened. Instead, he uses systematic desensitization to consciously and proactively decide to break this conditioning in himself. Before we go on and see how he does this, bear in mind that this process is never meant to be painful, scary, or unpleasant—quite the opposite! Rather, we are trying to create a new association, i.e., the trigger equals good feelings. This means that we cannot embark on the process feeling like we are being forced to do something we don't want to. Rather, remind yourself that you are in control, you go at the pace you want to, and that it's not supposed to hurt!

**Pick a Relaxation Technique**

The desired goal is to feel completely calm, content, and at ease with the stimulus/trigger. It should feel utterly neutral to you. Hence, you need a relaxation technique to create this feeling in yourself. There is no set way to create relaxed feelings, but there are several popular techniques you can choose from, and you can mix and match them or create your own. Here is a simple relaxation technique based on what's called progressive muscle relaxation.

1. Sit or lie down somewhere and begin with a few deep, slow belly breaths.
2. Start at your toes. Flex the toes upward as hard as you can, hold for a breath, and then relax. Flex them hard downward in the same way, hold, then release. As you release, do it slowly and with control, feeling the tension melt out of the muscles. You may like to repeat this a few times.
3. Move up your body and onto your calf muscles next. Flex them as tightly as you can, then slowly relax that tension as you breathe out.
4. Continue moving up your body, tensing and relaxing the muscles of the thighs, glutes, abdominal muscles, chest, shoulders, etc. It may be worth spending more time on the shoulders,

jaw, neck, and hands—the places we often hold most tension.
5. When you reach your face, pay individual attention to your lips, brow muscles, and forehead.
6. Now, as though your conscious were an illuminating spotlight, run your awareness over your body and see if you can find any spots of tension. If you do, zoom in there and repeat the tension/release and breathe deeply and slowly and then relax.
7. When you feel that your muscles are nice and relaxed, tell yourself "I am completely calm." These are not just words—really feel the sensation of calm in your body and what that's like. Become familiar with this state—you will need to find your way back here later!

Now, there are many, many variations on these breathing and relaxation techniques—it's not worth getting too hung up on exactly *how* you reach a state of calm, only that you reach it. Some people like to combine their muscle relaxation and breathing with mental imagery and visualization. If you found it useful to visualize in some of the techniques from previous chapters, you might find that it helps to incorporate them here.

For example, if you visualized your anxiety as the literal letters that spell out ANXIETY, made into a tall and foreboding brick wall, then you might like to imagine that this wall is being gently but steadily worn away by warm rain that makes the letters crumble and disappear.

Or take some time to construct your "happy place" in as much vivid detail as you can. It can be what you want—a remote paradise island with cool blue waters, a peaceful and dimly lit chapel, or a pink cloud floating far above the earth. The more familiar you are with this place and the more you make the connection that this place means relaxation, peace, and happiness, the easier you will be able to summon up the state of mind that comes with it. Remember that it's not the specific words, imagery, or technique that matters—what matters is that you are finding reliable paths into a calm state of mind.

## Construct Your Ladder

You will need to set up a program/plan for yourself. Be deliberate. How you do it is up to you, but make sure that you are genuinely challenging yourself and that each step on the ladder is a fairly consistent increase from the step before it. If the ladder isn't quite right, that's okay, too, though—you can always make adjustments. Nick's ladder looks like this:

1. Book a concert ticket
2. Mentally rehearse the steps needed to get to the concert and meet a friend there
3. Leave the house and walk to the subway station
4. Do the above but also get on the tube and travel to the right stop
5. Do the above but also walk around the busy streets in the city for around ten minutes
6. Repeat, but for thirty minutes
7. Stand in a busy crowd for ten minutes
8. Stand in a busy crowd for thirty minutes
9. Stand in a busy crowd for an hour or more

10. Talk to your friend and tell them about some of the difficulties you're experiencing

You may look at this ladder and think that step ten doesn't seem so bad, or that walking around the city is more stressful than lingering in a crowd. But so long as your ladder makes sense to you, then that's fine! To make your own ladder, you might find it helpful to first start by jotting down a whole bunch of different scenarios that cause you anxiety. Then, go through each one and sort them into piles: high, medium, and low. Then take each pile and try to rank them in order. You might need to break a few down into smaller tasks. Then, try to assign every task a number on a scale of one to ten. If it's more appropriate, you may find a scale of one to one hundred is better.

Nick starts his process by booking some concert tickets to a show he really wants to see, with a friend he has been neglecting somewhat. The show is in two months, giving him time to work through his ladder.

On his own terms, he works through the ladder. He buys the tickets, then pauses and immediately runs through his relaxation technique. He started out feeling a little anxious, but after relaxing, he felt better. He took the time to mark the milestone and praised himself, even if it is only a small step. Next, he runs through the other steps, one after the other. So, when he has worked his way up to step five, he walks around the city. When he feels his anxiety levels rising and his mood dropping, he pauses, finds a quiet corner, and quickly runs through a shortened version of the relaxation technique.

At step seven, he flounders a little and finds that he is overwhelmed, and comes home unhappy and defeated. That's okay. He stays at that level for some time. Whenever he encounters fear, sadness, shame, or any other negative emotion, he stops and runs through his relaxation protocol. This is important—he never "pushes through." The only condition for his moving up the ladder is that he is completely comfortable with the previous step.

Nick looks carefully at the task before him and his rough timeline and commits to taking a small step on the ladder every single day. Because he is deliberately trying to break old associations and create new ones, he takes the time after every session to go through affirmations, to recognize his progress, and to dwell on any good feelings he has managed to create. In two months' time, Nick finds the concert a challenge, but he attends and enjoys it. When he comes home, he feels so good and so proud of the progress he's made that he immediately creates a new ladder. Step one of this ladder is "go to another concert with my friend."

## Part 4: The Rewind Technique

In the final chapter of our book, we're going to explore a technique specifically designed to help with overcoming trauma. Post-traumatic stress disorder (PTSD) is a complex condition that is best dealt with by professionals, but as dedicated self-therapy practitioners, we can use some of the same techniques to help us better cope with our own traumas—whether we have a diagnosed trauma condition or not. The technique described below has much in common with systematic desensitization.

**The rewind technique originates from the field of neuro-linguistic programming (NLP), and when it was**

**initially developed, it was referred to as the visual kinesthetic dissociation technique**. One of the versions of the technique is taught by Dr. David Muss. In 1991, he contributed an article on the topic to the *British Journal of Clinical Psychology*. In this particular study, he used the rewind technique to treat nineteen law enforcement officers who were suffering from PTSD. Two years were spent monitoring the officers' every move. Astonishingly, all of the officers showed improvements in their trauma responses, and most importantly, none of them had a relapse after completing the program.

Let's have a look at how we can apply the practice in our own lives.

**Step 1: Identify a "Target Learning"**

This refers to the body responses that are caused by the trauma. For example, with the law enforcement officers, a frightening altercation with an armed assailant may leave someone with flashbacks to the event, intrusive thoughts, avoidance, insomnia, and nightmares. This is the target learning that can be rebooted and rewritten.

Remember, all of these symptoms have a physiological basis—trauma, like anxiety, begins in the nervous and endocrine system. The goal is then to make sure that these kinds of triggers no longer cause these kinds of physiological reactions. Instead, the technique helps you come up with more appropriate responses that fit the level of threat in the here and now.

## Step 2: Set Up a Mismatch Experience

Your nervous system responses happen whenever something reminds the brain of the traumatic event. In our example, having someone walk or move behind the law enforcement officer may instantly remind them of that terrifying situation. But as with systematic desensitization, we can create our own situations here in the present and condition a different set of responses.

Setting up a mismatch experience will make you feel safe. This is done by "reliving" the trauma, but in a way that doesn't overwhelm you, and then taking yourself back to a safe place. In our example, the "target learning" (in other words, the conditioned response or the mental association) is that people moving behind you equals danger.

You cannot change the past of what happened then, but what you can do is replay and rehearse a different outcome to the same experience. Creating a "mismatch" experience is where we create a moment where someone being behind us equals calm and neutral. Every time you rehearse this rewound experience, you are essentially training your neurochemistry, your endocrine system, and your mental associations to play out a scene differently.

**Step 3: Repeat the Mismatch**

The mismatch process is as follows:

1. Visualize the "safe place" before the incident
2. Watch yourself watching the TV screening of the traumatic event
3. Embody the movie and rewind quickly to the safe place

Let's take a closer look. Fully relaxing, you take your time imagining a calm and safe place in your mind's eye. As you do this, you are creating real physiological feelings of calm in your central nervous system. Now, *from within your safe space*, you then expose yourself to the trauma, but with some psychological distance— as an observer rather than a participant, you watch the event unfold on TV. In your safe space, literally picture a TV screen playing the trauma, and you're holding the remote control. If this still feels a little difficult, you could even watch yourself watching yourself on TV!

Imagine that the film on TV begins before anything bad happens. Let's say in our example that the police officers are entering a house without any fear or concern. Then, the bad event is played through step by step. Then, when it's finished, the person imagines pausing the film and floating into the screen where they are now experiencing it in first person point of view.

They imagine that, while they are embedded in the film this way, the scenario is rewound so that they experience themselves moving swiftly backward through the event. They experience the event but moving backward. They end up at the beginning of the scene where it was safe and before anything bad happened. For the police officer, this means seeing the assault running backward and seeing the assailant move away from him and run backward out of the house and away.

And that's it. Repeat this process, each time landing up in the place of safety, i.e., the moment before the bad thing happened. Remember to play through the story forward while at a comfortable, safe distance (i.e., watching the TV from afar), and play through it backward while you are embedded in the story, watching it through your own eyes.

Eventually the association of the trigger and trauma response begins to fade. You will no longer experience the same emotional reaction when faced with the trigger. Seems like magic, but it isn't. Instead, it simply confirms what scientists now know about how the brain responds to trauma and how that response can be "overwritten." Every time you rehearse this situation but reverse it, you are teaching your brain that it has a pleasant outcome, that it results in safety, and that it always ends in a neutral way. And your brain rewrites itself accordingly.

If the process is still successful, you will still remember the trauma and be able to look at it and talk about it, but you will no longer have the embodied physiological trauma response that you used to, the one that is so characteristic of PTSD.

The rewind technique works because it addresses every human being's need for "emotional checks and balances." When our need for safety is not met, mental health problems and especially PTSD can develop. **By reviewing and replaying traumatic events, you expose yourself to trauma but in a physically dissociative (i.e., defused) way, and so you eventually fade that emotional component.**

It may be helpful to seek out a trained therapist to guide you through this process, at least in the beginning. The great thing about this method is that you can practice the technique without ever having to reveal names or details of the trauma or having to recount the narrative to a therapist. You can try the technique on any event, long or short term, or practice it with many separate events and triggers, as is usually necessarily with CPTSD—complex PTSD.

The technique can help you stop involuntarily returning to traumatic memories and cut down on intrusive thoughts and flashbacks. It's as though your mind is given the opportunity to "put to bed" unfinished traumatic experiences, and the trauma response is rewritten and erased.

Take a look at the story of Katherine Vilnrotter from the website of the *Human Givens Institute*, which is a group of professional organizations and psychologists who believe that rewind therapy is a way to reboot some of the ingrained genetic "givens" we all start with in life. Says Katherine:

> *"We established that my calm, relaxing safe place would be a warm beach filled with sunshine and soft rolling waves. As Sue slowly counted to twenty with my exhales, I felt myself slip into a deeply relaxed state where I was fully conscious of everything happening around me.*
>
> *Sue's soothing voice then led me to a television set on the beach with a DVD player holding a DVD of my trauma experience. As soon as she mentioned the contents of the DVD, I was immediately transported back to it—I was there—and I instantly started crying and feeling the same life-threatening distress of the trauma. I had never accessed it so quickly before.*

*She brought me back to my relaxing beach to recover from the shock of feeling my naked emotions hit me so quickly. A few deep breaths later, I was ready to try again. [. . .] Sue took me through the rewind process. I saw myself watching the TV with the trauma playing forward and backward several times, but not actually seeing the screen. I then watched it play forward on the screen and I went backward through it.*

*As the memory was playing faster and faster, all I saw was a blur with particular moments as snapshots within it. I felt the distress on my face lessen and my breath normalize. After seeing it fly by countless times forward and backward, from various angles and points of view, I began to disconnect from it. My emotions were neutral, and I saw the trauma as a matter of fact and nothing else. After I had the pleasure of destroying the DVD in any way I wanted, Sue took me through scenarios that had triggered me in the past, describing my calm and confident reactions to them in the future.*

> *Sue then took the opportunity to remind me of positive aspects of my personality and my life accomplishments and reinforce the idea that I have the ability to realize my dreams.*
>
> *In short, it felt like she helped me remove the negative feelings and replace them with positive life-affirming feelings. After she brought me back to the room, I felt relaxed, happy, and emotionally exhausted."*

Again, it's important to seek out professional help if you're experiencing debilitating symptoms of PTSD or trauma. Though the above process is not difficult by any means, you may benefit far more from receiving tailored advice and support from a therapist who can adjust the technique to suit your unique situation.

**That said, you don't need to have a full-blown case of PTSD to benefit from the technique's power to essentially "rewind" situations**. We now know how influential certain life events can be on the core beliefs we develop, our self-concept, and the stories we tell ourselves. Clara, Thea, Nick, and Jamie all experienced their own individual patchwork of thoughts, feelings, expectations, biases, blind spots, shadows, secrets, habits, assumptions, hopes, dreams, fears, and difficulties. Most of these came directly from their early childhood experiences or by living through difficult events and relationships.

But what if these challenging situations were dealt with as and when they occurred, *before* they had a chance to embed themselves in the psyche as maladaptive thought patterns? Wouldn't it be nice to proceed through life with a continually updated and renewed psychological "clean slate"? If it seems appropriate to you, you can try combining the rewind technique with other approaches discussed here. Think of it as a kind of mental hygiene. Every time you experience a shock, a loss, a disappointment, an embarrassment, and so on, you pause and employ the rewind technique to take some of the neurochemical sting out of the experience.

The technique fits comfortably alongside positive visualization, calming and breathing techniques, opposite action, self-questioning, cognitive defusion, and even shadow work and reparenting. There's no reason you can't put memories from your earliest childhood on the TV, or watch from the security of your safe place possible future events that you might want to "cope forward" with. When you are your own self-therapist, you are empowered to use whatever techniques help you feel more self-empathy, more presence, and more awareness.

With heightened awareness, you can tell when you are having a physiologically anxious "fight or flight" response and can proactively choose to rewind through it again and again until the stimulus no longer produces that reaction. Your awareness lets you know how well your approach is working and gives you the confidence to adjust as you go, trusting in your own patience and consistency.

No two people are the same, and the challenges that each of us face are completely unique. Nobody can say what your journey to mental wellbeing will look like. But at the same time, no matter who you are, healing, coping, and resilience are all familiar human challenges, and they can *all* be met best with plenty of compassion, conscious awareness, and the courage to take action to make change.

**Summary:**

- Everyone encounters stress, disappointment, loss, and even trauma. Genuine resilience comes from knowing how to manage and cope. ACT's cognitive defusion is a way to gain psychological distance from overwhelming emotions so they can be managed. Distancing language, visualization, labeling, or the "leaves on a stream" exercise can help.
- We can *choose* how to relate to our thoughts and feelings in different situations. We can choose not to fuse, bond, or identify with transient sensations. We can accept thoughts without clinging to or resisting them or feeling compelled to react.
- "Coping ahead" is a DBT technique that lets us mentally rehearse and prepare for a challenging future event so we can cope better. We identify the potentially triggering situation, identify our skills and resources, then visualize and rehearse ourselves coping calmly, relaxing while we let our inner sage direct us.
- Systematic desensitization therapy is used to treat things like anxiety, phobias, OCD, and PTSD. By pairing graded

exposure with relaxation techniques, old conditioning and associations are broken and new ones formed.
- NLP's rewind technique is similar and helps combat PTSD by rebooting the neurochemical pathways of the traumatized brain. An association is identified and a mismatch experience set up, where the person dwells in a safe place while watching the traumatic memory play out as though on a TV. They then experience the situation again and again, but in reverse, so they land up in a place before the trauma happened.
- By reliving traumatic events, you expose yourself to trauma but in a physically dissociative way, and so you eventually fade the emotional component.

# Summary Guide

## CHAPTER 1: UNDERSTANDING THOUGHTS, BELIEFS, AND BEHAVIORS

- Many mental health problems come down to a **lack of awareness** of our own thoughts, feelings, and core beliefs. Being your own therapist requires the willingness to be honest, ask questions, and courageously take action according to the insights you glean.
- In CBT, we understand that not all thoughts are for our benefit, and that thoughts, feelings, and actions are all connected. What has been learned can be unlearned, and we can take automatic, negative, unhelpful, and unconscious thoughts and deliberately transform them into conscious, helpful ones that allow us to live the kind of lives we want to live.
- Using cognitive restructuring, we can rewrite or replace cognitive distortions, such as black-or-white thinking, catastrophizing, personalization, or

mindreading. We become aware, we appraise the accuracy and usefulness of a thought, and then we rewrite it.
- The behavioral activation theory approaches the problem on the behavioral level, telling us we need to act to feel better instead of waiting until we feel better to act. Monitor your routine, get in touch with your values and goals, then schedule activities that make you feel good, adjust and reappraising as you go.
- Core beliefs are deeply held ideas that influence how we behave, our self-identity, and our attitudes. Using the downward arrow technique, we keep asking questions to uncover our core beliefs, which can be changed.
- With the technique of opposite action, we engage fully in the exact opposite behavior of our initial emotional urge, and thus develop emotional regulation.

## CHAPTER 2: UNDERSTANDING WHAT YOU'RE MADE OF

- Self-therapy is about compassion but also about asking the right questions. The miracle question in particular asks us to imagine that the problem is already solved and to think about what that looks like. This helps us focus on solutions and possibilities. However, it's important to actually apply these insights and take appropriate action.
- Jung said the human "shadow" contains everything we don't accept in ourselves, but if we are able to tolerate all our emotions, we have a chance at wholeness and integration of all aspects of ourselves. We can pay attention to disproportionate emotional responses, embrace our imperfection, and take feedback on board, all without shame or blame.
- Avoidance mechanisms can help protect us until we're ready to process difficult material, but we should get in the habit of asking ourselves if there is something we are deliberately avoiding becoming aware of. Signs of this are avoidance, projection, reaction formation, escapism, etc. Instead of fleeing discomfort, become curious about the function its fulfilling.
- Gestalt therapy's empty chair technique is about addressing a person, idea, or

even part of the psyche as though it were sitting in an empty chair in front of you. This helps bring past patterns into the present so they can be processed. There are many variations, but all require an open, receptive mind and a non-directive attitude.

## **CHAPTER 3: WHERE IT ALL CAME FROM**

- If we want to know who we are now and why we are that way, we need to look at what came before, i.e., our childhoods. Bowlby outlined different styles of infant attachment (secure attachment, dismissive-avoidant, and fearful-avoidant) and showed how each shaped the adult's relationship patterns. We can become aware of and take responsibility for our attachment styles as adults, in the present. Working on self-esteem and having relationships with people with secure attachment styles are ways we can mitigate our early programming.
- You can also heal wounds from the past by "reparenting," which is consciously choosing to provide yourself as an adult

with everything you weren't provided with as a child. With visualization, our present-day adult goes back to engage with and heal their inner child. Become aware, conjure up the inner child, and dialogue with them, truly listening to what they say. Then commit to giving them what they need.
- It's important to apply the lessons learned in real life—for example, by setting boundaries or embracing healthier habits and routines.
- Eric Berne's transactional analysis is another way to understand our ingrained and stereotypical relationship patterns. Berne outlined three ego states we can occupy: parent, child, and adult. These unconscious patterns shape the "games" we play, but with conscious awareness, we can shift into a more neutral adult ego state.
- It's worthwhile asking yourself what role you most often play and what games recur in your life so that you can consciously choose something different.

**CHAPTER 4: ANXIETY, TRAUMA, AND COPING**

- Everyone encounters stress, disappointment, loss, and even trauma. Genuine resilience comes from knowing how to manage and cope. ACT's cognitive defusion is a way to gain psychological distance from overwhelming emotions so they can be managed. Distancing language, visualization, labeling, or the "leaves on a stream" exercise can help.
- We can *choose* how to relate to our thoughts and feelings in different situations. We can choose not to fuse, bond, or identify with transient sensations. We can accept thoughts without clinging to or resisting them or feeling compelled to react.
- "Coping ahead" is a DBT technique that lets us mentally rehearse and prepare for a challenging future event so we can cope better. We identify the potentially triggering situation, identify our skills and resources, then visualize and rehearse ourselves coping calmly, relaxing while we let our inner sage direct us.
- Systematic desensitization therapy is used to treat things like anxiety, phobias, OCD, and PTSD. By pairing graded exposure with relaxation techniques, old

conditioning and associations are broken and new ones formed.
- NLP's rewind technique is similar and helps combat PTSD by rebooting the neurochemical pathways of the traumatized brain. An association is identified and a mismatch experience set up, where the person dwells in a safe place while watching the traumatic memory play out as though on a TV. They then experience the situation again and again, but in reverse, so they land up in a place before the trauma happened.
- By reliving traumatic events, you expose yourself to trauma but in a physically dissociative way, and so you eventually fade the emotional component.

www.ingramcontent.com/pod-product-compliance
Lightning Source LLC
Chambersburg PA
CBHW030231100526
44583CB00013BA/786